America discovered by the Welsh in 1170 A.D.

Benjamin Franklin Bowen

AMERICA DISCOVERED

BY

THE WELSH

IN 1170 A.D.

BY

REV. BENJAMIN F. BOWEN.

Y Gwir yn erbyn y Byd

"The Truth against the World."

PHILADELPHIA:
J. B. LIPPINCOTT & CO.
1876.

PREFACE.

SOME time since, J. Sabin, the well-known book antiquarian of New York, related a very amusing story to me of a clergyman from Rhode Island coming into his store and inquiring whether he wished to purchase an Indian Bible. At once Mr. Sabin replied that he did, and that he would pay him five hundred dollars for it. The clergyman was delighted, returned to his home in Rhode Island, and, fearing to intrust so costly a relic to the express, determined to carry it himself to the city. With great eagerness he opened the book in Mr. Sabin's presence, when the latter, equally surprised and amused, exclaimed,—

"Why, sir, that's not an Indian Bible!"

"Not an Indian Bible!"

"Why, no, sir!"

The clergyman at first thought the antiquarian was quizzing him, but, seeing him so serious, asked,—

"Well, Mr Sabin, what makes you think so?"

"Because it is a *Welsh* Bible."

The clergyman hastily picked up the volume and disappeared.

The two languages bear a marked resemblance to each other. In the classification of the letters, the consonants in particular, including the gutturals, palatals, dentals, and labials, with their forms and mutations, hold such an identity in sound that any person not familiar with either language might take them to be the same, while he who understood both would as readily allow that in many respects they were akin.

The following pages are the result of an earnest desire to settle the question of, and, if possible, to fix the belief in, the voyages of Prince Madoc and his followers in 1170 A.D., and to assign them their rightful place in American history. Although this recognition has been very tardily given, by the almost utter silence of our historians, and the apparent unconcern of those linked with the Prince by blood, language, and country, the honor will be none the less real if bestowed now. Indeed, in this age of claims, and when every scrap of our general and local history is eagerly sought and read, it cannot be otherwise than that what is set forth in his favor will receive some share of attention from an intelligent public. Besides, so much earnest study has been given by those in other countries to the subject of the early discoveries on the American Continent, that it is hoped this contribution to its literature will serve to foster still further the spirit of inquiry, and be at the same time an acknowledgment of our debt to those countries for what they have furnished us in brain, heart, muscle, and life.

At intervals extending through several years, when released from the pressure of my public work, I have been engaged in the collection of the materials, both at home and abroad, from old manuscripts, books, pamphlets, magazines, and papers. The subject was not common, neither were the materials. What are the facts? That is the question. Facts of history, experience, observation. Speculative verbiage is avoided, for want of time and space. Others are made to take my place, for the sake of presenting what *they knew*. Such a method is more convincing than the expression of empty opinions.

B. F. B.

CONTENTS.

AMERICA DISCOVERED

BY

THE WELSH.

CHAPTER I.

THE MIGRATIONS OF THE WELSH

THE etymology of the names of persons, places, and things is a curious subject of inquiry. It is one of the safest guides in an attempt to distinguish the race-differences of a people whose history reaches back to an immemorial era.

The names of *Wales* and the *Welsh* are comparatively of recent origin. The Welsh have always called themselves Cymru or Cymry,—Romanized into Cambria or Cambrians. This has been the generic name of the race as far back as any trace can be found of their existence. The Romans changed Gal into Gaul; the Welsh sound *u* as *e*: hence they pronounced the Romanized word Gaul as Gael. The Saxons, as was their wont, substituted *w* for *g:* hence, as the people of Cambria were esteemed to be analogous to the Gauls, they called their country Waels or Wales, and its people Waelsh or Welsh; and these names have continued to the present time. But this people always have called themselves "Y Cymry," of which the strictly literal meaning is *aborigines.* They call their language "Y Cymraeg,"—the primitive tongue. Celt, meaning a covert or shelter, and Gaul, meaning an open plain or country, are terms applied to various subdivisions by which the Cymric race have been known. In this connection it may be appropriate to say that the word "Indian" is one that does not apply or belong to the red race of the American Continent, but was used by Columbus, who, anxious to discover the East Indies by a northwest route, imagined that he had reached that country, and called the inhabitants Indians. Subsequent events have proved his mistake. The primitive races of this continent are more properly designated by the word aborigines, as in the case of the Cymry.

Through the rich and copious language and literature of Wales, the student of history is able to gather a vast store of knowledge respecting its inhabitants and their early ancestors. The substantial result arrived at as to their origin and migrations may be briefly stated as follows:

First. That the inhabitants of Wales, known to Homer as the Cimmerii, migrated thither from the great fountain-head of nations,—the land of the Euphrates and Tigris.

Second. That they went in successive bands, each in a more advanced state of civilization than the former.

Third. That they carried with them a peculiar language, peculiar arts and superstitions, marking their settlement on the Island of Britain at a very early period.

Fourth That their journey through Europe is marked with the vestiges of tumuli, mounds, skulls, rude utensils, ornaments, and geographical names in their language.

The Welsh language is of a pure radical construction, and remarkably free from admixture with other tongues It is as copious, flexible, and refined as it was two thousand years ago, when it existed alongside the Greek and Latin, both of which it antedates and survives, for it is not, like them, a dead language, but is in living use at the present day in literature, commerce, home, and worship.

"'Dim Saesenaig! Dim Saesenaig!'" exclaimed the astonished Thomas Carlyle, when visiting the vale of Glamorgan, "'Dim Saesenaig!' (No English! No English!) from every dyke-side and house comes. The first thing these poor bodies have to do is to learn English."

Thomas Carlyle was greatly mistaken, if he ever believed that the Welsh would tamely surrender their Cymraeg. It has been the symbol of their unconquerable hope, and they watch with jealous care any inroads made upon it. Upon the principle that might is right, nations have been forced from their own soil, but with a most passionate tenacity they have still clung to their native tongue. True, there have been languages which have become extinct, like the nations which have spoken them, by conquest; but the Welsh continues to exist, because either the people who speak it have never been conquered, or it has proved itself superior to conquest.

Edward the First is supposed to have directed the final blow towards crushing Welsh independence; and yet there is at present preserved in the cathedral of St. Asaph, North Wales, the celebrated Rhuddlan Parliament Stone, on which is written this inscription :

This Fragment is the Remains
Where Edward the First held his
Parliament A.D 1283; in which the
Statute of Rhuddlan was enacted
Securing to the Principality of Wales
Its Judicial Rights and Independence.

The Welsh have a property in the British Isle which no earthly power can wrest from them. Henry the Second once asked a Welsh chieftain, "Think you the rebels can withstand my army?" He replied, "King, your power may to a certain extent harm and enfeeble this nation, but the anger of God alone can destroy it. Nor do I think in the day of doom any other race than the Cymry will answer for this corner of the earth to the Sovereign Judge"

Many centuries have elapsed since these brave and hopeful words were uttered, and the destiny of Wales is more manifest,—that her nationality will be swallowed up or merged with English laws, customs, and habits. still her language and literature will survive, and the names will continue fixed to assert the antiquity and greatness of her people. More than half the names borne by the population of England are of Cymric origin or derivation. More than three-fourths of the names in Scotland, and about one-half of those of France, are from the same source. Cambrian names are found all through Europe,—in Italy, Switzerland, Holland, Germany, and about the Pyrenees.

The Welsh name for London is *Llundain.* It was Latinized into *Lundinum*, and Anglicized into Lundon or London. Its etymology is from *llyn*, a pool or lake, and *Dain* or *Tain* for *Thames* (the sound of *d* being like that of *t*): hence, a pool or lake on the Thames. The low flat on the east side of London, known as "The Isle of Dogs," now a part of the mainland, was at one time flooded by the Thames; and hence the name of *Llundain*, or *Thames Lake.* Liverpool came from *Flowing Pool;* that is, the tide flowed in and out.

Avon is the generic Welsh name for river: hence Avon-Clyde, Avon-Conwy, Avon-Stratford. Cumberland stands for Cymbri-land, Northumberland for North Cymbri-land. *Aber* is the mouth of a river, Anglicized into *harbor:* hence there is Aber-Conway, Aberdeen. There is scarcely a river, mountain, or lake in England or in Scotland the etymology of which is not found in the Welsh language at the present day.

The ancient British language, physique, skull, hair, eyes, and flexure of pronunciation still preponderate in England, notwithstanding the incessant boasts of the Saxon, who was a barbarous savage when he arrived, and who did not exhibit a single instance of knowledge and learning until after he had come in contact with the Cymric race.

With a view to tracing the migrations of this race throughout Europe, observe the ancient geographical terms, with their strong physical traits.

Caucasus is derived from the two Welsh words *cau*, to shut up, to fence in, and *cas*, separated, insulated. This mountain-chain has borne this name from the earliest human records; and how expressive of their position and character, to inclose Europe from Asia!

The Caspian Sea means, when derived, *cas*, separated, and *pen*, head; literally, a sea with a head or source, but insulated and without an outlet. Any one familiar with this body of water can understand the force of the words.

Crimea comes from the Welsh word *crymu* (pronounced kri'me, the *c* being sounded as *k*, and the *u* as *e*), which means to bend or curve; literally, a circular peninsula. The Crimea was the Gwlad yr Haf (summer land) of the Cymry.

Alps is derived from *al*, grand, sublime, and *pen*, head,—a sublime head.

Armorica comes from *ar-y-môr*, upon the sea.

Danube finds its derivation from *dan*, under, below, and *uf* (pronounced *uv* or *ub*), spreading or diffused. Some of the Cymric bands or colonies, in their migrations westward, halted along the banks of the Danube; others settled on the Elbe, and were called the Wendi, and their descendants speak at the present time a slightly-corrupted Welsh language Bautzen, in Bavaria, and Glogau, in Prussia, are old Cymric towns; and an eminent German scholar has shown what ancient Cymric relics are to be found in the museums of Dresden and Berlin. Recently many learned philologists were excited into a sharp discussion to account for the name of the German capital, Berlin Its origin is plainly Cymric, and is derived from *ber*, a curve, and *lin*, a river.

There is such a striking resemblance between the ancient Cymric laws, as compiled by Dyfnval Moelmud, and the Institutes of Menu, that many of the most able Oriental and Welsh scholars have concluded that another branch of the Cymric race must have gone eastward from the Caucasus and penetrated into India. Sir William Jones, a son of a Welshman, translated these Institutes of Menu, or Brahminic Laws, and says, "The name '*Menu*' is clearly derived from *menses*, *mens*, or mind, as all the Pandits agree that it means intelligent." *Menw* in Welsh means the seat of intelligence.

Moreover, it is generally admitted that the Welsh contains a sufficient number of root-words by which the original connection of the Semitic (Hebrew, Chaldee, Syriac, Egyptian, etc) and the Indo-European languages is distinctly shown. And, as will be subsequently proved, a large number of words have been found in use by the aborigines of the American Continent, whose roots or simplest forms were related to roots of words in the old languages, many of which were directly connected with the Cymric tongue.

The object of this cursory sketch has been to show that, from the very earliest period, the branches of the Cymric race have been extensively spread over the earth, as indicated by the sure testimony of their language, that they moved from east to west, preceding all other races—the Teutonic, Sarmatian, etc.—by long intervals of time From the certain data of history these things are placed beyond doubt,—by Herodotus, Cæsar, and others Would it be surprising, then, if, in accordance with the same nomadic principle and these westward migrations, together with the fierce persecutions of the northern hordes, some portions of the Cymry were driven still farther westward and were wafted to the American Continent?

CHAPTER II

BY WHOM WAS AMERICA FIRST PEOPLED?

By whom and by what means the American Continent was originally peopled has been, in the main, an unsolved problem. That it will always remain so does not appear from new proofs which are being adduced to support favorite theories. Four of these theories have, at different times, and with much intelligent zeal, been maintained

(1.) That the ancestors of the American aborigines came from Europe,—that they were Caucasians, but became changed in color by the use of red roots and the bleachings of the sun; and of these were represented the Romans, Grecians, Spaniards, Irish, Norsemen, Courlanders, Russians, and Welsh.

(2.) That they came from Asia, and comprised Israelites, Canaanites, Assyrians, Phœnicians, Persians, Tartars, East Indians, Chinese, and Japanese.

(3.) That they came from Africa, the original cradle, it is maintained, of the American aborigines, who are made the descendants of the Egyptians, Carthaginians, or Numidians.

(4.) That the American aborigines are the descendants of all the nations in the world.

The last is certainly the most accommodative, and can be made to bend to suit the shifting exigencies of an imperfect state of knowledge. The skeptical view would not be accepted, inasmuch as it broke the unity of the race,—namely, that all the original people and animals of America were distinct creations.

Beginning with Peleg, whose name signifies division, when Noah divided the earth between his sons, Shem, Ham, and Japheth, there is found a basis for the repeopling of the earth. Africa was assigned to Ham, the temperate zones to Shem, and the frigid zones to Japheth. Heathen altars and the mounds of early Scripture are taken as the original types of the earthen monumental remains of America. At the dispersion on the plains of Shinar, and after the confusion of tongues, "the Lord scattered them abroad from thence upon the face of *all* the earth" It was the opinion of Ogilby, cosmographer to the English king in 1671, that men and animals came soon after the flood from Armenia to Tartary, and thence, by continuous land-route by way of the present Behring Straits, to America.

The Atlantis of Homer, Solon, Plato, and Hesiod, which was supposed to unite the continents of Africa and America, or which was a great island situated between them, seems to lose, by time, more of its mythical character, and to be brought to the plane of a historic fact It certainly cannot be treated as a pure fiction. The story that Solon brought from Egypt to Greece of the Atlantic island was not new there; for a great festival was held in Greece, accompanied with symbols, to show what advantage the Athenians had in their wars with the Atlantes.

Diodorus Siculus (book v chap ii) seems to refer to America in the following: "Over-against Africa lies a very great island in the vast ocean, many days' sail from Libya westward The soil is very fruitful. It is diversified with mountains and pleasant vales, and the towns are adorned with stately buildings." He then alludes to the Phœnicians sailing along the Atlantic coast of Africa. The theory that the land forming the bed of the Atlantic Ocean between Brazil and Africa is a vast sunken tract is hardly defensible. The remnants of Cape Verd and Ascension Islands, and the numerous rock-formations and sand-banks surveyed with great accuracy by Bauche, have been submitted in its favor. Traditions exist that a people on the Mediterranean, sailing through the Straits of Gibraltar, the ancient Calpe, were driven westward by a storm, and were heard of no more. It is thought they reached the American coast. Some time since, at a meeting of the Mexican Geographical Society, it was stated that some *brass tablets* had been discovered in the northern part of Brazil, covered with Phœnician inscriptions, which tell of the discovery of America five centuries B.C.

They are now in the museum of Rio Janeiro. They state that a Sidonian fleet left a port of the Red Sea, rounding the Cape of Good Hope, and following the southeast trade-winds until the northeast trade-winds prevented farther progress north, and they were driven across the Atlantic The number of the vessels, the number of the crews, the name of Sidon as their home, and many other particulars, are given.

It is given as veritable history that a farmer near Montevideo, South America, discovered in one of his fields, in 1827, a flat stone which bore strange and unknown characters; and beneath this stone was a vault made of masonry, in which were deposited two ancient swords, a helmet, and a shield. The stone and the deposits were brought to Montevideo, and most of the inscriptions of the former were sufficiently legible to be deciphered. They ran as follows:

"*During the dominion of Alexander, the son of Philip, King of Macedon, in the sixty-third Olympiad, Ptolemais.*"

On the handle of one of the swords was a man's portrait, supposed to represent Alexander. The helmet had on it fine sculptured work, representing Achilles dragging the corpse of Hector around the walls of Troy. This would seem to point to an early Grecian discovery of America.

Humboldt cites a passage of Plutarch, in which

he thinks that both the Antilles and the great continent itself are described.

In "Varia Historia," book iii. chap. xviii., Ælian tells how one Theopompus relates the particulars of an interview between Midas, King of Phrygia, and Silenus, in which the latter reported the existence of a great continent beyond the Atlantic, "larger than Asia, Europe, and Libya together."

In 1761, Deguignes, a French scholar, made known to the world that the Chinese discovered America in the fifth century. He derived his knowledge from Chinese official annals. He affirmed that in the year 499 A.D., Hoei Shin (Universal Compassion), a Chinese Buddhist priest, returned to Singan, the capital of China, and declared that he had been to Tahan (Kamtschatka), and from thence on to a country about twenty thousand *li* (short Chinese miles), or about seven thousand English miles. The measurements are taken to be about the distance between China and California, or Mexico. He called the country Fusang, from the name of an abundant plant,—the Mexican "maguey," or American aloe.

He described the gold, silver, copper, and other ores which abounded; also the customs, rites, and cycles of time; and these are made to agree with what has been known of the American aborigines. Oriental scholars, like Klaproth and Bretschneider, have handled these pretensions with keen severity; while there have not been wanting others who allege that the Japanese and Chinese do not record myths. There is a description of Fusang in the Japanese Encyclopædia,—Wa-kan-san-taï-dzon-yé.

Abbé Brasseur de Bourbourg says, in his "Popol Vuh," a book on the ancient people of Mexico and Central America, "There is an abundance of legends and traditions concerning the passage of the Irish into America, and their habitual communication with that continent, many centuries before the time of Columbus. We should bear in mind that Ireland was colonized by the Phœnicians An Irish saint, named Vigile, who lived in the eighth century, was accused to Pope Zachary of having taught heresies on the subject of the antipodes. At first he wrote to the Pope in reply to the charge, but afterwards went to Rome in person to justify himself, and there proved to the Pope that the Irish had been accustomed to communicate with a transatlantic world."

Brereton's account of Gosnold's voyage to the New England coast in 1602 mentions an occurrence off the coast of Maine, of his having met "eight Indians, in a Basque shallop, with mast and sail, an iron grapple, and a kettle; that they came aboard boldly, one of them being appareled with a waistcoat and breeches of black serge, made after our sea-fashion, hose and shoes on his feet: all the rest (saving one that had a pair of breeches of blue cloth) were naked"

Michel, in his "Les Pays Basques," thinks that

the Basques, being adventurous fishermen, were accustomed to visit the American coast from time immemorial. They were engaged in the whale and other fisheries.

The voyages of the Norsemen, and their temporary settlements on the American Continent, are now too well authenticated to admit of any doubt.

In the preceding chapter it was shown that the Welsh were a migratory race, and had moved from the lands of the Euphrates and Tigris in an eastward direction, and also westwardly, till, in the time of Homer, they occupied the British Island. They were surrounded by water. Their very necessities made them navigators. They conducted large fisheries. The Phœnicians and Greeks traded with them in tin and lead, and in the Baltic for amber. Their commercial relations were extensive before Julius Cæsar reached the island. He came to attack and subdue them, because their naval power, as he himself says, assisted the Gauls. Their ships were made of oak, and were so strong as to be impenetrable to the beaks of the Roman ships, and so high that they could not be annoyed by the darts of the Roman soldiers.

King Canute, in the eleventh century, had vessels with sixty rowing-benches. Early voyagers traversed seas and oceans with comparative safety Though they had not the compass (which, by the way, is uncertain), they studied the elements of nature,—the winds, currents, sun, and stars. Modern sailors have the advantage of accurate instruments to reduce their observations. The ascensions and descensions of the sun by day, and the polar star by night, are sufficient guides to prevent sailing wide of points.

Between America and Europe are two great currents,—the southwesterly bearing towards the former continent, and the northeasterly towards the latter. The majestic Gulf Stream sweeps around from Newfoundland till it almost crosses the Atlantic near the British Island. That is why the steamship-lines adopt the course of sailing-vessels. By the aid of the simple forces of nature, early voyagers reached the American Continent.

CHAPTER III.

THE VOYAGES OF PRINCE MADOC.

OWAIN GWYNEDD was esteemed one of the greatest princes Wales ever produced

Upon the death of his father, which occurred in 1137 A D, he took his share of the possessions, which were divided, according to the custom of the nation, among the sons, and he ruled North Wales, his seat of government being at Aberfraw, till 1169 A.D, when he died.

Gwalchmai, a Bard of his times, addressed to him the following spirited ode in celebration of an important victory he achieved over the English at the battle of Tal y Moelvre:

"The generous chief I sing of Rhodri's line,
With princely gifts endow'd, whose hand
Hath often curb'd the border land,
Owain, great heir of Britain's throne,—
Whom fair Ambition marks her own,
Who ne'er to yield to man was known,
Nor heaps he stores at Avarice's shrine

"Three mighty legions o'er the sea-flood came,
Three fleets intent on sudden fray;
One from Erin's verdant coast,
One with Lochlin's armèd host,
Long burdens of the billowy way;

The third, from far, bore them of Norman's name,
To fruitless labor doom'd, and barren fame.

"'Gainst Mona's gallant lord, where, lo! he stands,
His warlike sons ranged at his side,
Rushes the dark tumultuous tide,
Th' insulting tempest of the hostile bands:
Boldly he turns the furious storm,
Before him wild Confusion flies,
While Havoc rears her hideous form,
And prostrate Rank expiring lies,
Conflict upon conflict growing,
Gore on gore in torrents flowing,
Shrieks answering shrieks, and slaughter raving,
And high o'er Modore's front a thousand banners waving.

"Now thickens still the frantic war;
The flashing death-strokes gleam afar,
Spear rings on spear, flight urges flight,
And drowning victims plunge to night;
Check'd by the torrent-tide of blood,
Backward Menai rolls his flood,
The mailed warriors on the shore,
With carnage strew'd, and dyed with gore,
In awful anguish drag their mangled forms along,
And high the slaughter'd throng
Is heap'd, the King's red chiefs before.

"Lloegria's onset thus, Lloegria's flight,
The struggle doom'd her power to tame,
Shall, with her routed sons, unite
To raise great Owain's sword to fame;
Whilst sevenscore tongues of his exploits shall tell,
And all their high renown through future ages swell."

Many other odes are extant in the Welsh language, written in honor of this great prince, which have never been surpassed in true poetic spirit, elegance of diction, and metrical ease, by the productions of any other country.

Owain Gwynedd had nineteen children. The names of the sons were Rhodri, Cynoric, Riryd, Meredydd, Edwal, Cynan, Rien, Maelgon, Llewelyn, Iorweth, Davydd, Cadwallon, Hywell, Cadell, Madoc, Einon, and Phylip; and of this number Rhodri, Hywell, Davydd, and Madoc were the most distinguished.

Iorweth, being the eldest son, was entitled to succeed his father, but was declared unfit to occupy such a position, on account of an injury done to his nose, which gained for him the not very euphonious name of Drwyndwn (Swarthy-nose).

Hywell was a brilliant soldier and poet, and many of his best productions are still preserved. His mother was a native of Ireland, and although not born in wedlock, thus being regarded as an illegitimate son, he aspired to the crown after the death of his father, and succeeded in obtaining it, at the same time granting to Iorweth the cantrevs of Nanconwy and Ardudwy.

Soon after, he went to Ireland to receive possession of his mother's property, but upon his return he found Davydd, the legitimate son of Owain by another wife, asserting in arms his right to the throne under the sanction of a legitimate birth. The consequence was that the entire country became embroiled in a bitter civil war. Hywell was slain in battle, and Davydd ab Owain occupied his father's throne As a stroke of perfidy, or policy, he married the sister of King Henry the Second, whereby he succeeded in breaking for a time the independent spirit of the Welsh. He gave aid to his brother-in-law in money and men, and attended the Parliament at Oxford. Such a treacherous course excited the disgust and hatred of his brothers, as well as of his subjects generally, so that his realm continued in a state of wild revolt and dissension. Davydd, suspicious and alarmed lest he might lose his throne through some unforeseen intrigues, seized and imprisoned Rhodri, slew Iorweth, and drove his other brethren into exile.

He was so intractable in spirit, and so cruel, that he put out the eyes of large numbers who were not subservient to his will.

From all the concurrent evidences which can be gleaned, it appears that Madoc was the commander of his father's fleet, which at that time was so considerable as successfully to oppose that of England at the mouth of the Menai in the year 1142. The poem in which Gwalchmai has celebrated this victory has already been given in this chapter. There is also an allusion to it in Caradoc's History, p. 163, 4th ed., 1607.

Madoc was of a mild, gentle temperament, and must have felt deeply grieved at the unnatural dissensions existing between his own brothers. Moreover, he was an object of suspicion himself, exposed to his brother Davydd's ferocity, who imagined that he might also dispute the question of succession to the throne. Doubtless it was this that led Madoc to resolve that he would leave those scenes of contention, and seek, in exile from his native country, some other land in the west, if such could be found Being commander-in-chief of the fleet, he was able to take a speedy departure.

This emigration of Prince Madoc seems to have been commemorated by Bards who lived very near the time in which it took place. According to various old documents, his enterprise of exploring the ocean westward resulted in the discovery of a new world, from which he returned to make known his good fortune and to gather other emigrants to accompany him thither. He accordingly fitted out a second expedition, and, taking his brother Riryd, Lord of Clocran in Ireland, with him, they prevailed upon a number to accompany them, sufficient to fill ten ships. They set sail from a small port, five miles from Holyhead, in the island of Anglesea.

There is a large book of pedigrees still extant, written by Jeuan Brecva, who flourished in the age preceding the time of Columbus, where the above event is thus noticed in treating of the genealogy of Owain Gwynedd: "Madoc and Riryd found land far in the sea of the west, and there they settled."

The Bards were the historians of those times. By a perusal of the compositions of those who were contemporary with Madoc, it is found that his name is mentioned three or four times by Cynddelw, Llywarch, and Gwalchmai. These are held to be among the most celebrated of the Welsh Bards. Their works, which are mostly extant in manuscript, would each of them make a respectable volume.

Llywarch, who was the son of Llewelyn, wrote a poem while undergoing the ordeal of the hot iron to prove his innocence respecting Madoc's death. He invoked the aid of the Saviour "lest he should injure his hand with the shining sword and his kinsmen should have to pay the *galanas*" It is addressed

"TO THE HOT IRON.

"Good Iron! free me from the charge
Of slaying. Show that he
Who smote the prince with murderous hand
Heaven's kingdoms nine shall never see,
Whilst I the dwelling-place of God
Shall share, safe from all enmity."

The same poet, in a panegyric, addressed to Rhodri ab Owain Gwynedd, of Hywell and Madoc, his brothers, says,—

"Two princes were there, who in wrath dealt woe,
Yet by the people of the earth were loved:
One who in Arvon quench'd ambition's flame,
Leading on land his bravely toiling men,
And one of temper mild, in trouble great,
Far o'er the bosom of the mighty sea
Sought a possession he could safely keep,
From all estrangéd for a country's sake"

In a poem addressed to Prince Llywelyn ab Iorweth by the same bard, there appear the following lines:

> "Needless it is to ask all anxiously,
> Who from invaders will our waters guard?
> Llywelyn, he will guard the boundary wave;
> The lion i' the breach, ruler of Gwynedd.
> The land is his to Powys' distant bounds,
> He met the Saxons by Llanwynwy lake,
> Across the wave is he victorious,
> Nephew of Madoc, whom we more and more
> Lament that he is gone"

Gwalchmai addressed an ode to Davydd ab Owain Gwynedd, lamenting his being deprived of that prince's brothers:

> "Silent I cannot be without mentioning who they were,
> Who so well of me merited praise·
> Owain the fierce, above the muse's song,
> The manly hero of the conflict;
> Cadwallon, ere he was lost,
> It was not with smooth words he praised me;
> Cadwaladyr, lover of the harmony of exhilarating songs,
> He was wont to honor me;
> Madoc, distributing his goods,
> More he did to please than displease me."

In an elegy on the family of Owain Gwynedd, by Cynddelw, Madoc is twice mentioned, one passage particularly seeming worthy of attention:

> "And is not Madoc by the whelming wave
> Slain? How I sorrow for the helpful friend!
> Even in battle was he free from hate,
> Yet not in vain grasp'd he the warrior's spear."

There is a Welsh triad entitled "The Three Losses by Disappearance." The first loss was that of Gavran, the son of Aeddan Vradog, a chieftain of distinguished celebrity of the latter part of the fifth century. He went on an expedition to discover some islands which are known by the name of Gwerddonan Llion, or the Green Islands of the Ocean. He was never heard of afterwards, and the situation of these islands became lost to the Welsh.

The second loss was that of Merddin, who was the Bard of Emrys Wledig, or the Ambrosius of Saxon history, by whose command Stonehenge was erected.

Merddin is held as one of the three Christian Bards of Wales,—Merddin Wyllt and Taliesin being the other two.

This Merddin, with twelve Bards, went to sea, and they were heard of no more.

The third loss of this remarkable triad was Madoc ab Owain Gwynedd, who, with three hundred men, went to sea in ten ships, and it is not known whither they went.

About 1440 A.D., Meredydd ab Rhys, having obtained the loan of a fishing-net by a poem, sent a second poem with it when he returned it, and wrote thus:

"Let Ivan, of a generous stock,
Hunt, like his father, on the land,
In good time, on the waters, I,
By liberal aid, will hunter be.

> Madoc the brave, of aspect fair,
> Owain of Gwynedd's offspring true,
> Would have no land,—man of my soul !—
> Nor any wealth, except the seas
> Madoc am I, who, through my life,
> By sea will seek my wonted prey"

Madoc was a navigator, and made the sea his home. No doubt can be entertained on that point. In the above quotation the poet likens himself to Madoc as the true type of a sailor.

It has been said that the Welsh Bards were historians. They were retained in families of importance to record the actions of their ancestors and those of the Bards themselves in odes and songs. While they may have employed a poetic license in their construction, the facts themselves were not lost out of sight. So far as can be known, it appears that these odes were written prior to any definite notion of a Western world, known subsequently as the American Continent. Madoc's voyages might not have been very familiar to many except the Welsh, and they were ignorant whither he went. One thing, however, is absolutely certain, that this tradition having existed for centuries could not have been invented, as some have suspected, to support the English against the Spanish claims of prior discovery. A period of three hundred and twenty-two years intervened between that of Madoc and that of Columbus.

CHAPTER IV.

SUPPORTED BY WELSH AND OTHER HISTORIANS.

MANY valuable historical documents in prose and in poetry relating to the Welsh nation were destroyed by the order of Edward the First of England about the time that he so inhumanly massacred the Welsh Bards. He feared that their recitations of patriotic poetry among the people might serve to awaken and preserve the spirit of liberty and independence among them, and lead eventually to their casting off the yoke he was so cruelly imposing upon them.

Sir John Wynne, who was born in 1553 and died in 1626, wrote the history of the Gwedir family, which remained in manuscript until published by Hon. Daines Barrington in 1773. It contains an enumeration of the various branches of the descendants of Owen Gwynedd, especially those who were claimed to be the more immediate ancestors of Sir John's family. He mentions Madoc as the son of Owen Gwynedd, but makes no reference to his voyages. He touches upon the subject of the massacre of the Bards by Edward the First, "who," he says, "caused them all to be hanged by martial law as stirrers-up of the people to sedition" Some of the records of Welsh history were removed from their usually secure retreats in abbeys to London, as testified to by Sir John and others, particularly William Salesbury, who declared that they were burned, "and that there escaped not one that was not incurably maimed, and irrecuperably torn and mangled"

This happened in the Tower, where, previous to their destruction, many of the political prisoners from Wales obtained leave to read "such books of their tongue as they most delighted in."

In view of these facts, and considering that the history of the events contemporaneous with the period at which Madoc is alleged to have left his native land is unusually scanty on this subject, it is more than probable that some of these lost manuscripts contained particular accounts of Madoc's departure. Fortunately, however, enough has escaped the spoiler's hand to furnish such proof to every rational mind that the question must be regarded as settled.

Caradoc, of Llancarvan, Glamorganshire, wrote, in his native language, a history of Wales He lived at the time Owen Gwynedd was in the height of his power and fame, and was familiar with all the more important events in connection with his country. His history was translated into English by Humphrey Lloyd, and published by Dr. David

Powel in the year 1584, and has been reprinted several times since In it is contained the following narrative, which bears all the semblance of historical truth that any narration of facts can. Its plainness, naturalness, and simplicity are at once evident:

"On the death of Owain Gwynedd, Prince of North Wales, about the year 1169, several of his children contended for his dominions; and Madoc, one of his sons, perceiving his native land engaged, or on the eve of being engaged, in a civil war, thought it best to try his fortune in some foreign clime. Leaving North Wales in a very unsettled state, he sailed, with a few ships which he had fitted up and manned for that purpose, to the westward, leaving Ireland to the north. He came at length to an unknown country, where most things appeared to him new and uncustomary, and the manners of the natives far different from what he had seen in Europe. Madoc, having viewed the fertility and pleasantness of the country, left the most part of those he had taken with him behind (Sir Thomas Herbert says that the number he left behind was one hundred and twenty), and returned to North Wales. Upon his arrival he described to his friends what a fair and extensive land he had met with, void of any inhabitants, whilst they employed themselves and all their skill to supplant one another for only a ragged portion of rocks and mountains. Accordingly, having prevailed with considerable numbers to accompany him to that country, he sailed back with ten ships, and bid adieu to his native land." There is an apparent contradiction between "the manners of the natives" and "void of inhabitants." The historian meant to convey the idea by the latter phrase that the portion Madoc discovered was thinly peopled, and might be occupied without much difficulty.

But it is conjectured that Caradoc's writings do not reach any lower than the year 1157,—which would be thirteen years earlier than the time of Madoc's departure, or 1170 Some suppose that Caradoc must have died in 1157, because the *Brut* or Annales from which Humphrey Lloyd chiefly compiled his history of Cambria, and which bore Caradoc's name, did not extend beyond that year. There is no sound reason for this belief: many of the various *Bruts* bore his name, and it is altogether likely that he was living when Madoc set sail and returned, prior to his final leave. It would not be wise, however, to dispute Humphrey Lloyd, Caradoc's translator into English, who says that that part of the history beyond 1157, and, of course, that including Madoc's voyages, was compiled from collections made from time to time, and kept in the abbeys of Conway in Carnarvonshire, North Wales, and Strata Florida, Cardiganshire, South Wales. These and other abbeys were the repositories of literature and history for many centuries, whose registers were carefully compared together every third year, when the Beirdd or Bards belonging to these houses went on their customary visitations, which were called *clera*. This practice continued until the death of Prince Llewelyn, or a little prior, about the year 1270. If Caradoc did not continue his history beyond 1157, and that because of his death in that year, even then there is no reason to question the veracity of those monks of Conway and Strata Florida who continued the same history in their registers Guttun Owen, a Bard in the reign of Edward the Fourth of England, about the year 1480 obtained one of the most perfect copies of these registers. He doubtless had special facilities, since he was personally commissioned by Henry the Seventh to search the pedigree of Owen Tudor, that king's grandfather, among the Welsh annals. Another Bard about the same time with Guttun Owen mentioned this event. His name was Cynfrig ab Gronow. Thus, step by step, for the space of three hundred years, can be traced through Bards and historians this recital respecting Madoc, and all prior to the discovery of America by Columbus; so that it cannot possibly be said that the claims afterwards advanced in favor of Madoc were an after-thought.

Rev. Josiah Rees, the editor of a Welsh magazine published in Wales in 1770, told the Welsh scholar Edward Williams that he had in his possession at that time two or three fair manuscripts of Caradoc of Llancarvan, with the continuation by the monks of Strata Florida, Guttun Owen, and others. He furthermore said that he had compared these originals with Dr Powel's translation, or, more strictly speaking, with Humphrey Lloyd's translation, which Dr Powel published in 1584. Mr. Rees said that it was the most faithful he ever met with in any language Lord Lyttleton, in the last century, then, was very much mistaken, and withal quite ignorant, when he said that Dr Powel "dressed up some tradition concerning Madoc in order to convey an idea that his countrymen had the honor of first discovering America" Dr. Powel himself did not entirely depend on Lloyd's translation in the preparation of the work for the press, for he says that he compared that translation with the original records, and therefore was able to correct his copy. All this proves that Caradoc's history, with the continuation from the registers of Conway and Strata Florida, the writings of Guttun Owen, Cynfrig ab Gronow, Sir Meredyth ab Rhys, and others, were extant in the days of Lloyd and Powel, and consequently these two latter historians would have been detected if they had been in any degree guilty of misrepresentation or forgery

In Hakluyt's "Collection of Voyages," a large and costly edition published in 1589, there is found, in connection with other important statements, the following:

"After the death of Owen Gwynedd, his sons fell at debate who should inherit after him; for the eldest son born in matrimony, Iorweth, or Edward (Drwyndwn), was counted unmeet to govern, because of the maim upon his face, and Howel, that took upon him the rule, was a base son, begotten upon an Irishwoman. Therefore David, another son, gathered all the power he could, and came against Howel, and, fighting with him, slew him, and afterwards enjoyed quietly the whole land of North Wales until his brother Edward's son [Llewelyn] came to age.

"Madoc, another of Owen Gwynedd's sons, left the land in contentions betwixt his brethren, and prepared certain ships with men and munition, and sought adventures by seas, sailing west, and leaving the coast of Ireland so far north that he came to a land unknown, where he saw many strange things. This land must needs be some part of the country of which the Spaniards affirm themselves to be the first finders since Hanno's time (the Carthaginian admiral, supposed to have flourished about four hundred and fifty years before Christ); whereupon it is manifest that that country was by Britons discovered long before Columbus led any Spaniards thither.

"Of the voyage and return of this Madoc there be many fables framed, as the common people do use, in distance of place and length of time, rather to augment than to diminish; *but sure it is, there he was.* And after he had returned home and declared the pleasant and fruitful countries that he had seen, and, upon the contrary, for what barren and wild ground his brethren and nephews did murder one another, he prepared a number of ships, and got with him such men and women as were desirous to live in quietness, and, taking leave of his friends, took his journey thitherwards again.

"Therefore it is supposed that he and his people inhabited part of those countries; for it appears by Francis Lopez de Gomara that in Acuzamil, and other places, the people honored the cross. Whereby it may be gathered that Christians had been there before the coming of the Spaniards; but, because this people were not many, they followed the manner of the land which they came to, and the language they found there. This Madoc, arriving in that western country, unto the which he came in the year 1170, left the most of his people there, and, returning back for more of his own nation, acquaintance, and friends to inhabit that fair and large country, went thither again with ten sails, *as I find noted by Guttun Owen.* I am of opinion that the land whereunto he came was some part of the West Indies."

It is worthy of observation that Hakluyt distinctly says that he derived his account from Guttun Owen, and, therefore, from the original sources themselves, as it has been shown that Owen secured perfect copies from the abbeys. Hakluyt does not refer to Lloyd and Powel as his authorities, because he was fortunate in gaining access to the writings from which they too had compiled their histories. Thus the historical veracity of Lloyd and Powel is, without design, sustained by the learned Hakluyt.

Another point that should not be passed is in relation to the last sentence of the extract just given, wherein Hakluyt expresses his opinion that Madoc touched the West Indies. It will be understood that during the earlier discoveries that name —West Indies—embraced not only those islands which are now known by it, but also so much of the continent or mainland as had been occupied.

During the reign of Queen Elizabeth, who ascended the throne in 1558, the belief seems to have been universal that Madoc did sail and discover America; and most historical writers of the time have introduced the subject into their writings with the same credence that any other well-ascertained fact deserves.

Hornius, in his "De Originibus Americanis," gives an account of the same event. The following is an extract translated from the Latin:

"From hence he [Hakluyt] concludes that Madoc, with his Cambrians, discovered a part of North America. A cursory attention to the figure of the earth must convince every one that on this direction he must have landed on that continent; for beyond Ireland no land can be found except Bermuda to this day [1650] uncultivated but the extensive continent of America. As Madoc directed his course westward, it cannot be doubted but that he fell in with Virginia or New England, and there settled.

"Nor is this contradicted by its being said that the country was uninhabited and uncultivated; for that country is very extensive, and in our times, after six centuries, is but thinly peopled Besides, that tract on which Madoc landed might be desert, and yet other places in the interior parts, possessed by the barbarous Chichimecas, might be populous, with whom the Cambrians mingled, and, the communication being dropped between them and their mother-country, they adopted the language and manners of the country. The traditions prevailing among the natives strongly confirm me in this opinion; for the Virginians and Guahutemallians, from ancient times, worshipped one Madoc as a hero. Concerning the Virginians, see Martyr, decade vii chap. 3, concerning the Guahutemallians, decade viii. chap 5. Among them we have Matec Zungam and Mat Ingam; and why this should not be Madoc the Cambrian, whom the monuments in the country prove to have been in those parts, no reason can be given. As to antiquity, five centuries are sufficient, beyond which American traditions do not ascend."

In another part he says, "For when it is demonstrated that Madoc, a prince of Cambria, with some of his nation, discovered and inhabited some lands in the West, and that his name and memory are still retained among them, scarcely any doubt remains."

Peter Martyr, alluded to in the above extract, lived in the court of Ferdinand, King of Spain. He was the author of several works, among them the "Decades," which contain the references to Matec Zungam, or Madoc the Cambrian. He was at court when Columbus returned from his first voyage, and is considered good authority with respect to what he wrote about in those times. He distinctly affirms that some nations in America honored the memory of one Madoc when Columbus landed on that coast.

Our next quotation will be from "Letters writ by a Turkish Spy," who lived forty-five years undiscovered in Paris, giving an impartial account to the Divan at Constantinople of the most remarkable transactions of Europe from the year 1673 to 1682. They were originally written in Arabic. The author of this work, which caused a great sensation at the time, as well from the highly-interesting character of its contents as from the profound secrecy in which the name of the writer was long involved, was John Paul Maiana, a native of Italy. He says, "This prince [Charles II.] has several nations under his dominions, and it is thought he scarce knows the just extent of his territories in America. There is a region on that continent inhabited by a people whom they call Tuscorards and Doegs. Their language is the same as is spoken by the Welsh. They are thought to descend from them. It is certain that when the Spaniards first conquered Mexico they were surprised to hear the inhabitants discourse of a strange people that formerly came thither in corraughs, who taught them the knowledge of God and immortality, instructed them also in virtue and morality, and prescribed holy rites and ceremonies of religion. 'Tis remarkable, also, what an Indian king said to a Spaniard, viz., that in foregoing ages a strange people arrived there by sea, to whom his ancestry gave hospitable entertainment, in regard they found them men of wit and courage, endued also with many other excellencies, but he could give no account of their original or name. The Welsh language is so prevalent in that country that the very towns, bridges, beasts, birds, rivers, hills, etc., are called by Welsh names. Who can tell the various transmigrations of mortals on earth, or trace out the true originals of any people?"

Sir Thomas Herbert visited Persia and many other countries about 1626, and in connection with his travels mentioned Madoc's emigration to the West. He states that Madoc embarked at Abergwilly, and first reached Newfoundland, whence, coasting along, he in time came to a convenient place for settlement; that, after recruiting the health of his men, and fortifying the spot he had pitched upon, leaving a hundred and twenty of his crew, he returned to Wales, and conducted back to his new home a fleet of ten barks, and found but few of those he left remaining. With the aid of Einon and Idwal, he soon put things in order again, and waited vainly for the arrival of other emigrants from Wales, of those who were to have followed him; but none came, owing to the wars with England. Sir Thomas concludes by saying that "had this voyage of the Prince of Gwynedd been known and inherited, *then had not Columbus, Americus Vespucius, Magellan, nor others, carried away the honor of so great a discovery, nor had Madoc been defrauded of his memory, nor our kings of their just title to a portion of the West Indies.*"

CHAPTER V.

THE NARRATIVE OF REV. MORGAN JONES.

In the year 1740 there appeared in the "Gentleman's Magazine," London, England, a very remarkable narration, written by Rev. Morgan Jones. It is as follows:

"These presents may certify all persons whatever, that in the year 1660, being an inhabitant of Virginia, and chaplain to Major-General Bennet, of Mansoman County, the said Major Bennet and Sir William Berkeley sent two ships to Port Royal, now called South Carolina, which is sixty leagues to the southward of Cape Fair, and I was sent therewith to be their minister. Upon the 8th of April we set out from Virginia, and arrived at the harbor's mouth of Port Royal the 19th of the same month, where we waited for the rest of the fleet, that was to sail from Barbadoes and Bermuda, with one Mr. West, who was to be Deputy Governor of said place. As soon as the fleet came in, the smallest vessels that were with us sailed up the river to a place called the Oyster Point. Here I continued about eight months, all which time being almost starved for want of provisions, five others, with myself, travelled through the wilderness till we came to the Tuscarora Country. Here the Tuscarora Indians took us prisoners, because we told them that we were bound to Roanoke. That night they carried us to their town, and shut us up close, to our no small dread. The next day they entered into a consultation about us, which after it was over, their interpreter told us that we must prepare ourselves to die next morning. Whereupon, being very much dejected, and speaking to this effect in the British tongue: Have I escaped so many dangers, and must I now be knocked on the head like a dog? then presently an Indian came to me, which afterwards appeared to be a war-captain belonging to the sachem of the Doegs (whose original I find must needs be from the old Britons), and took me up by the middle, and told me in the British tongue I should not die, and thereupon went to the Emperor of the Tuscaroras, and agreed for my ransom and the men who were with me. They then welcomed us to their town, and entertained us very civilly and cordially four months, during which time I had the opportunity of conversing with them familiarly in the British language, *and did preach to them three times a week in the same language*, and they would confer with me about anything that was difficult therein. At our departure they abundantly supplied us with whatever was necessary to our support and well-doing. They are settled upon Pontigo River, not far from Cape Atros [Hatteras]. This is a brief recital of my travels among the Doeg Indians

"MORGAN JONES,

"Son of John Jones, Basaleg,

near Newport, County of Monmouth.

"I am ready to conduct any Welshmen or others to the country

"NEW YORK, March 10, 1685-6."

It appears that the origin of this narration came about in the following way, as described by Charles Lloyd, Esq., of Dôl y Frân, Montgomeryshire, in a letter which he has written He says, "My brother, Dr. Thomas Lloyd, of Philadelphia, Pennsylvania, having heard of Rev. Morgan Jones's adventures, and meeting him in New York, desired him to write them out with his own hand in his house; and to please me and my cousin, Thomas Price, of Llanvyllin, he sent me the original. Mr. Jones was living then within twelve miles of New York, and was contemporary with me and my brother at Oxford. He was of Jesus College, and called there 'Senior Jones,' by way of distinction."

The original was given to Dr. Thomas Lloyd, and transmitted to his brother, as mentioned above; subsequently it came into the possession of Dr. Robert Plott, through Edward Lloyd, A.M., keeper of the Ashmolean Museum at Oxford, the former having maintained in his writings his implicit belief in Madoc's emigration and Mr. Jones's narrative. Rev. Theophilus Evans afterwards communicated the narration to the "Gentleman's Magazine" He was a Welsh clergyman, vicar of St. David's in Brecon, and well versed in the history of his nation. It is to be regretted that other accounts of the travels of Mr. Jones among the Doegs of the Tuscaroras, which were published at an earlier period, have not been preserved, inasmuch as they would materially assist in more fully establishing the veracity of the writer. As it is, however, it does not appear that his truthfulness has ever been questioned. He was an educated man, a graduate of Oxford, and not likely to be mistaken or led into an easy credulity. He is explicit as to the mode of his rescue, while engaged in prayer and deploring his wretched fate, the time he remained among them, his conversing with them and explaining anything difficult between them,—nothing unreasonable to expect, after the lapse of so many centuries,—his preaching to them three times a week All these things, taken in connection with his accurate description of the location of this tribe, must impress the candid reader that this clergyman gave a recital of unvarnished facts.

At the time Mr. Jones was captured, the Tuscaroras inhabited a range of country that extended from Virginia down into the Carolinas. They comprised several branches, known as Doegs, Chowans, Meherrins, and Nottoways, who dwelt along the rivers bearing some of their names. They were often called the Southern Iroquois, because they were chiefly kindred in dialect with the main body of that mighty confederacy, the Five Nations, or Iroquois proper. They made frequent incursions into the territory of the Carolinians, by whom they were severely defeated in 1712: large numbers were taken prisoners, while the remainder fled northward and formed the sixth nation of the celebrated Iroquois Confederacy. Iroquois was a term applied to this confederacy by the French; Mingoes was the name given to those composing it by the great Algonquin race of red men, by whom they were largely surrounded, and with whom they were almost incessantly engaged in bloody and decimating wars.

The Five Nations called themselves Konoskioni, or "Cabin-Builders." The territory they occupied when Europeans obtained a more general acquaintance with them, which embraced New York, Pennsylvania, Ohio, Virginia, and portions of the Carolinas, evidently had not been in their possession a very great length of time. From all that can be ascertained, they came from the west, in an easterly direction, crossing the Nauraesi Sipu (Mississippi), and made war upon another nation, called the Alligewi or Alleghanians, destroyed their works, and drove them into the interior, the conquerors taking possession of the eastern country. Now, who were these Alligewi? That they were expelled from the lands held by the Five Nations there can be no doubt; that they moved westward is equally certain But who were they? They were supposed to be whites. McCulloh, in his "Researches on America," says that an exterminating war appears to have taken place between the barbarous natives (Iroquois) and their more refined and civilized neighbors, ending in the nearly total destruction of the latter, the few survivors of whom fled to happier climes, and to these aboriginal whites, perhaps, the Mexicans were indebted for their refinement and knowledge. Traces of these Alligewi are found throughout those portions of the country of the Eastern States once held by them, afterwards by Iroquois. Their line of march westward may be clearly traced by the earthen fortifications they threw up for purposes of defence against their savage and wily enemies. Almost without exception the traditions of the red men ascribe the construction of these works to white men. Some of them belonging to different tribes at the present say that they had understood from their prophets and old men that it had been a tradition among their several nations that the eastern country and Ohio and Kentucky had once been inhabited by white people, but that they were mostly exterminated at the Falls of Ohio. The red men drove the whites to a small island (Sandy Island) below the rapids, where they were cut to pieces. *Kentuckee*, in Indian, signifies *river of blood* Some of the fragments of the ancient tribe of the Sacs expressed astonishment to a gentleman at St. Louis that any person should live in Kentucky. The country, they said, had been the scene of much blood, and was filled with the *manes* of the butchered inhabitants, who were white people.

The westward movements of the tribes which were overpowered and displaced by the Iroquois are distinctly marked, and show that a European civilization had some influence in directing the construction of those lines of defences along the largest valleys and streams of the countries through which they passed, until, arriving at the Ohio, they made a vigorous stand, with the resolution not to be driven any farther into the interior. This will account for the much greater number of earthen defences found along the Ohio, and, besides, agrees with the traditions of the red men. When, however, defeated here, after a residence extending over many years, the remnants of those tribes which survived the bloody battles fled up the Missouri.

But who were these Alligewi, or Alligenians? The word is strikingly familiar to the Welsh ear, with its double *l*, and corresponds with the Welsh words *alli*, mighty, and *geni*, born, or "mighty born."

Although the Tuscaroras, among whom Mr. Jones lived and preached, were supposed to be akin to the Iroquois in language and finally confederated with them, it is altogether probable that they were more anciently a branch of the Alligewi, who could not be driven from their soil These Tuscaroras were lighter in color than the other tribes, and so noticeable was this peculiarity that they were generally mentioned as *White Indians.* Emanating from this source, many travellers subsequently applied the title to tribes through whose boundaries they passed in the West and South. Doubtless they had a common origin

They stated that their ancestors were Welsh If the objection is made, how they could have lost traces of European civilization so soon, it may be recollected that the buccaneers of St. Domingo had in thirty years forgotten all knowledge of Christianity. Such radical differences as exist between the white and red races could not have been lost without the lapse of centuries; while their languages would undergo, more or less, some marked modifications. Dr. Williams, writing upon this subject in his "Enquiry," published in 1791, says, "When it is considered that Mr Jones's visit to these nations was nearly five hundred years after the emigration of Prince Madoc, it can be no wonder that the language of both Mr. Jones and the Indians was very much altered. After so long a period, Mr. Jones must have been obliged to make use of words and phrases in preaching Christianity with which they must have been altogether unacquainted. Besides, all living languages are continually changing: therefore, during so many centuries, the original tongue must have been very much altered, by the introduction of new words borrowed from the inhabitants of the country. Though the language was *radically* the same, yet Mr. Jones, especially when treating of abstract subjects, was hardly intelligible to them without some explanations. We are told that the religious worship of the Mexicans, with all its absurdities, was less superstitious than that of the ancient and learned Greeks and Romans. May we not conclude that the Mexicans derived some part of their religious knowledge from a people enlightened by a Divine revelation, which, though very much corrupted in the days of Madoc, yet was superior to heathen darkness?"

Many of the names mentioned by Mr. Jones in his narrative seem to have a Welsh origin, and bear a precisely similar sound to words in that language

Pontigo—a name applied to a river in that country where he found them—seems derived from Pont y Go, "The Smith's Bridge," or Pant y Go, "The Smith's Valley;" a smith dwelling beside a river or bridge being sufficient to originate such a name. Dr. Robertson says, in his "History of America," vol. ii. p. 126, that "the Indians were very ignorant of the use of metals; artificers in metals were scarce, and on that account a name might be given to a bridge or valley where one dwelt." Doeg Indians might be a corruption of Madog's Indians. The majority of those who have had any convictions on this subject have believed that Madoc first landed with his colony somewhere in New England, and that they then moved down the coast and inhabited portions of the country between Virginia and Florida. New England has some vestiges of European civilization which were there before the Pilgrim Fathers landed. The celebrated round tower at Newport, Rhode Island, about the origin of which tradition and history are silent, is certainly constructed on the same principle as Stonehenge, England, and many other Cambrian memorials. It conforms exactly to the Druidic circle. Its materials are unhewn stone. It rests upon eight round columns, twenty-three feet in diameter, and twenty-four feet in height. Any person familiar with Cambrian and Scandinavian archæology will not hesitate to attribute the construction of this tower rather to the Cambrian than to the Scandinavian navigators.

A letter written by Charles Lloyd, Esq., of Dôl y Frân, in Montgomeryshire, already mentioned, published in 1777 by Rev. N. Owen, jun., A.M., in a pamphlet entitled "British Remains," strongly confirms Mr. Jones's narrative, and the truth of Madoc's voyages.

Mr. Lloyd says that he had been informed by a friend that a Mr. Stedman, of Breconshire, about thirty years before the date of his letter, was on the coast of America in a Dutch bottom, and being about to land for refreshment the natives kept them off by force, till at last this Stedman told his fellow Dutch seamen that he understood what the natives spoke. The Dutch bade him speak to them, and they were thereupon very courteous; they supplied them with the best things they had, and told Stedman that they came from a country called Gwynedd (North Wales), in Prydain Fawr (Great Britain). Prydain was the son of Hugh the Mighty, and supposed to have been the first to establish government and set up royalty in the isle of Britain, and the island was called by his name. Mr. Lloyd said that Mr. Stedman found these Welsh Indians along the coast between Virginia and Florida. Furthermore, this gentleman said that a Mr. Oliver Humphreys, a merchant, who died not long before the date of Mr. Lloyd's letter, told him that when he lived at Surinam he spoke with an English privateer, or pirate, who, being near Florida, careening his vessel, had learned, as he thought, the Indian language, which his friend said was perfect Welsh.

It is to be regretted that Rev. Morgan Jones and these others could not have given more of the traditional history of these Indians; but what they have recited is explicit. Here is no collusion, no attempt to meet the tradition concerning Madoc, for they, in all probability, knew nothing about it

If the Welsh Indians could be identified as descendants of Madoc's colony, or if the Alligewi could be ascertained to have been the Welsh, the discovered traces of civilization, Christianity, and the arts might partly be referred to their instrumentality. They may have contributed to swell the tide of population, and aided in constructing those forts and works which so much resemble those of their own country. Our American mounds agree in the minutest particulars with those described by Pennant as found during his "Tour in Wales."

This is the opinion of De Laet, Hornius, Mitchel, and others.

CHAPTER VI.

THE NARRATIVE OF REV CHARLES BEATTY.

IN a "Journal of a Two Months' Tour," written by Rev. Charles Beatty, A.M., and dedicated to the Earl of Dartmouth, London, 1768, the author presents a sketch of a visit to some of the inland parts of North America during the year 1766. He was accompanied by a Mr. Duffield. Mr. Beatty was a missionary from New York, and travelled several hundred miles in a southwest direction from that city. During his tour he met several persons who had been among the Indians from their youth, or who had been taken captives by them and lived with them several years.

When at the foot of the Alleghany Mountains, Pennsylvania, he stopped at the house of Mr. John Miller, where he met with one Benjamin Sutton, who had been taken captive by the Indians, had been in different nations, and had lived many years among them. He informed Mr. Beatty and his companion that "when he was with the Choctaw nation or tribe of Indians, at the Mississippi, he went to an Indian town a very considerable distance from New Orleans, whose inhabitants were of different complexions,—not so tawny as those of the other Indians,—and who spoke Welsh. He said that he saw a book among them, which he supposed was a Bible, which they kept carefully wrapped up in a skin, but they could not read it; and that he heard some of these Indians afterwards in the lower Shawanese town speak Welsh with one Lewis, a Welshman, who was a captive there. This Welsh tribe now live on the west side of the Mississippi, a great way above New Orleans"

At Tuscarora Valley—a name, be it remembered, the same as that of the tribe among which Rev. Morgan Jones found those speaking Welsh —Mr. Beatty met with another man, named Levi Hicks, who had been a captive from his youth. He said that he "was once attending an embassy at an Indian town on the west side of the Mississippi, where the inhabitants spoke Welsh (as he was told, for he did not understand them); and our Indian interpreter, Joseph Peepy, said he once saw some Indians, whom he supposed to be of the same tribe, who talked Welsh. He was sure that it was Welsh, for he had been acquainted with Welsh people and understood some words.

"Mr. Sutton farther told us that he had often heard the following traditions among them; that of old time their people were divided by a river, and one part tarrying behind; that they knew not for certainty how they first came to this continent, but account for their coming into these parts near where they are now settled; that a king of their nation left his kingdom to his two sons; that the one son making war upon the other the latter thereupon determined to depart and seek some new habitation; that accordingly he set out accompanied by a number of his people, and that after wandering to and fro for the space of forty years they at length came to the Delaware River, where they settled, three hundred and seventy years ago. The way, he says, they keep an account of this is by putting a black bead of wampum every year since on a belt they had for that purpose. He farther added that the king of that country from whence they came, some years ago, when the French were in possession of Fort Duquesne (Pittsburg), sent out some of his people in order, if possible, to find out that part of their nation that departed to seek a new country, and that these men, after seeking six years, came at length to the Pickt Town, on the Ouabache River, and there happened to meet with a Delaware Indian named Jack, after the English, whose language they could understand; and that by him they were conducted to the Delaware towns, where they tarried one year, and returned; that the French sent a white man with them, properly furnished, to bring back an account of their country, who, the Indians said, could not return in less than fourteen years, for they lived a great way toward the setting sun. It is now, Sutton says, about ten or twelve years since they went away"

Dr. Williams, who wrote upon this subject, thought that these traditions referred to the unsettled state of North Wales, the departure of Madoc, and his travels before he finally settled.

It would not be surprising if Mr. Beatty's Indian interpreter, Joseph Peepy, had been among Welsh people in Pennsylvania, for large colonies of Welsh settled, in early colonial days, in and around Philadelphia. "The Welsh Tract" is still well known. William Penn and his family were of Welsh extraction. A large number of his followers were Welshmen. Philadelphia contains a larger proportion of Welsh descendants than any other city in the United States. The first mayor of the city, Anthony Morris, and the first Governor of the colony of Pennsylvania, Thomas Lloyd, were both Welshmen.

These colonies extended more and more into the interior, and came in contact with the nearest tribes. Traffic was carried on between them, and in this way Mr. Beatty's interpreter became somewhat acquainted with the Welsh tongue. Afterwards, penetrating far into the interior, where he spent many years, he found, as he informed Mr. Beatty, Indians speaking the same language he had heard among the Welsh people of Pennsylvania. To his testimony is added that of Benjamin Sutton and Levi Hicks, each independent of and consistent with the other. By means of these, and others, the residents of Pennsylvania were made acquainted with the existence of Welsh Indians. It is not at all likely that all, if indeed any, of them then knew of the historical records in Wales relating to Madoc; it was afterwards that they found out there were such.

The Rev. Thomas Jones, of Nottage, in the county of Glamorgan, came to America in 1737. His son, Samuel, was then about three years of age. He gave him a liberal education in Philadelphia, where he took the degree of Doctor of Divinity. He, (Dr) Samuel Jones, wrote a letter to Rev. William Richards, of Lynn, in Norfolk. In that letter, speaking of the Madocian Indians, he says, "The finding of them would be one of the most pleasing things to me that could happen I think I should go immediately amongst them, though I am now turned fifty-five; and there are in America Welsh preachers ready to set out to visit them as soon as the way to their country is discovered. I know now several in Pennsylvania who have been amongst those Indians"

The following words are in a letter from Mr. Reynold Howells to a Mr. Mills, dated Philadelphia, 1752: "The Welsh Indians are found out: they are situated on the west side of the great river Mississippi."

William Pritchard, a bookseller and printer of Philadelphia, when in London, in 1791, told some

Welsh scholars, among them Mr. Owen and Dr. Williams, that he had often heard of the Welsh Indians, that in Pennsylvania they were universally believed to be very far westward of the Mississippi, that he had often heard of people who had been among them, and that if he should be but very little assisted he should immediately visit them.

A writer in the "Mount Joy Herald," after alluding to Powel's "History" upon this subject, which has been quoted already, gives this additional extract from the same:—"Three hundred and twenty-two years after this date,—Madoc's departure,—when Columbus discovered this continent a second time and returned to Europe to make his report, it caused great excitement, and he was justly applauded. But his enemies, and those who envied his fame, boldly charged him with acquiring his knowledge from the charts and manuscripts of Madoc In the year 1854 I had a conversation with an old Indian prophet, who styled himself the fifteenth in the line of succession. He told me, in broken English, that long ago a race of white people had lived at the mouth of Conestoga Creek, who had red hair and blue eyes, who cleared the land, fenced, plowed, raised grain, etc., that they introduced the honey-bee, unknown to them He said the Indians called them the Welegcens, and that in the time of the fifth prophet the Conestoga Indians made war with them, and, after great slaughter on both sides, the white settlers were driven away. Our fathers and grandfathers used to tell us what a hatred and prejudice the Conestoga Indians had against red-haired and blue-eyed people in all their wars in Eastern Pennsylvania When taking white prisoners, they would discriminate between the black-haired and the red, showing mercy to the former, and reserving the latter for torture and death. This would seem to indicate that they knew from tradition of Prince Madoc and his followers, and of the fearful fight they had made.

"About the year 1800 (for I must quote from memory), a man digging a cellar in the vicinity of the Indian Steppes came upon a lot of small iron axes, thirty-six in number. My father, who resided in Manor township and followed blacksmithing, was presented with one of these relics; and I recollect seeing it in his shop twenty-five years after that date. It was curiously constructed; the eye was joined after the fashion of the old garden hoe; it had no pole end, and had never been ground to an edge, nor had the others ever been. It had lain so long in the ground that the eye was almost eaten through with rust; and its construction was so ancient that I looked upon it as the first exodus from the stone to the iron axe."

Rev Morgan Jones, of Hammersmith, England, wrote a letter to Dr. John Williams, in which he says that his father and his family went to

Pennsylvania about the year 1750, where he met with several persons whom he knew in Wales,—one in particular with whom he had been intimate. This person had formerly lived in Pennsylvania, but then lived in North Carolina. Upon his return to Pennsylvania, the following year, to settle his affairs, they met a second time. Mr Jones's friend told him that he then was very sure there were Welsh Indians, and gave as a reason, that his house in North Carolina was situated on the great Indian road to Charlestown, where he often lodged parties of them. In one of these parties, an Indian, hearing the family speak Welsh, began to jump and caper as if he had been out of his senses Being asked what was the matter with him, he replied, "I know an Indian nation who speak that language, and have learnt a little of it myself by living among them;" and when examined, he was found to have some knowledge of it. When asked where they lived, he said, "A great way beyond the Mississippi." Being promised a handsome reward, he said that he would endeavor to bring some of them to that part of the country; but Mr. Jones, soon after returning to England, never heard any more of the Indian

In the "Gentleman's Magazine" for July, 1791, page 612, Mr. Edward Williams says that about twenty years prior he became acquainted with a Mr. Binon, of Coyty, in the county of Glamorgan, who had been absent from his native country over thirty years. Mr. Binon said he had been an Indian trader from Philadelphia for several years; that about the year 1750 he and five or six others penetrated much farther than usual to the westward of the Mississippi, and found a nation of Indians who spoke the Welsh tongue. They had iron among them, lived in stone built villages, and were better clothed than the other tribes. They gave Mr. Binon a kind reception, but were suspicious of his companions, taking them for Spaniards or Frenchmen, with whom they seemed to be at war. They showed him a manuscript book, which they carefully kept, believing that it contained the mysteries of religion, and said *that it was not long since a man had been among them who understood it.* This man, whom they esteemed a prophet (could it have been the Rev. Morgan Jones?), told them, they said, that a people would some time visit them and explain to them the mysteries contained in their book, which would make them completely happy. They very anxiously asked Mr. Binon if he understood it, and, being answered in the negative, they appeared very sad, and earnestly desired him to send some one to them who could explain it. After he and his fellow-travellers had been for some time among them, they departed, and were conducted by those friendly Indians through vast deserts, and were supplied by them with plenty of provisions, which the woods afforded; and after they had been brought to a place they well knew, they parted with their numerous Indian guides, who wept bitterly on their taking leave, and very urgently entreated them to send a person to them who could interpret their book. On Mr. Binon's arrival in Philadelphia, and relating the story, he found that the inhabitants of the Welsh Tract had some knowledge of these Indians, and that some Welshmen had been among them. He also learned then that on several occasions parties of thirty and forty of these Welsh Indians had visited the Welsh settled on the Tract near Philadelphia. Mr Binon furthermore said that when he told those Indians, whom he had visited, that he came from Wales, they replied, "It was from thence our ancestors came, but we do not now know in what part of the world Wales is."

Mr. Edward Williams, who gave to the world the above account from Mr. Binon, also had an interview with a Mr. Richard Burnell, a gentleman who went to America about the year 1763, and who returned to England when the American war broke out.

During Mr. Burnell's residence in and near Philadelphia, he became well acquainted with the Welsh people, who informed him that the Welsh Indians were well known to many in Pennsylvania. He personally knew Mr. Beatty, whose narrative opens this chapter, and a Mr. Lewis, who saw some of these Welsh Indians in a congress among the

Chickasaws, with whom and the Natchez Mr. Burnell says they are in alliance. He also said that there was in Philadelphia a Mr. Willin, a very rich Quaker, who had obtained a grant of a large extent of country on the Mississippi, in the district of the Natchez; and, having taken with him a great number of settlers, he had among them Welshmen who understood the Indians. Mr. Burnell, anxious to be informed, waited upon Mr. Willin, who assured him that among his colony there were two Welshmen who perfectly understood the Indians and would converse with them for hours together, and that these Welshmen had often assured him the Indians spoke the Welsh language; that some of them were settled in those parts, some on the west side of the Mississippi, and others in remote parts. At this time Mr. Burnell had a son, Cradog Burnell, settled at Buck's Island, near Augusta, Georgia He was a capital trader in the back settlements. A company of about a hundred persons had purchased forty millions of acres from the Natchez and Yazoos along the Mississippi and the rivers Yazoo and Tombecbe, which fall into it. Mr. Burnell's son was connected with this large colony; and he said that probably his son knew more about these Welsh Indians "than any man living. He had the best opportunities, for he reads and writes the Welsh language extremely well."

If it be granted that Mr. Binon saw a manuscript book among those whom he visited, and that neither they nor he could read it, that would not be surprising; for many persons of greater intelligence in these times cannot read old books in the manuscript or old-style print of centuries ago. Most of them were written in the Roman character; but there are some in the Greek character, which, transferred to the Welsh or old English, would demand scholarship to interpret.

Let it be borne in mind, too, that the time is not very far back when it was considered quite an accomplishment for kings and queens to be able simply to read. There are books in manuscript and print in the public libraries of the world, dating back many centuries, which cannot be read and understood by those in whose vernacular they were written or printed.

Enough recitals have been added to the narrative of Rev. Charles Beatty to render it absolutely certain that in his time and during his tour through Pennsylvania there existed a firm conviction, based on personal knowledge and experience, that there was a tribe of Indians who spoke the Welsh language, that they formerly had occupied the eastern portions of the country, but, pressed by their enemies, red and white, they had retreated farther and farther into the interior, and had become broken into scattering fragments, incorporating themselves in some cases with other tribes Can they be pursued by the antiquary or the historian? Let the succeeding pages answer

CHAPTER VII.

THE WELSH INDIANS MOVING WEST.

MODERN investigations and discoveries show that there once existed an almost unbroken system of defences, extending from New York, Pennsylvania, Virginia, and the Carolinas, in a diagonal direction, to the valley of the Ohio, and thence into the great basin of the Mississippi. These works increase in size and number as they advance towards the centre, and may properly be classified into forts for defence and tumuli or mounds for sepulture. They are chiefly found along the fertile valleys through which run large rivers, and at their junctions with one another. It is quite usual with writers on these remarkable works to assign to them so great an antiquity that the employment of figures is almost useless if they tell the truth. But there are substantial reasons for the belief that they were erected by the Welsh, aided by those Indians with whom they became incorporated and whom they directed in their labor. The route they took, either by choice or necessity, and the exact correspondence of these earthen monuments with those found in England and Europe known to be of Cambrian origin, go very far to support this belief

In Onondaga, New York, there are vestiges of ancient settlements dating back beyond the time when the council-fires of the Six Nations burned there. These are protected by three circular forts.

Isaac Chapman, Esq, says, in his "History of Wyoming," Pennsylvania, "In the valley of Wyoming there exist some remains of ancient fortifications, which appear to have been constructed by a race of people very different in their habits from those who occupied the place when first discovered by the whites. Most of these ruins have been so obliterated by the operations of agriculture that their forms cannot now be distinctly ascertained. That which remains the most entire was examined by the writer during the summer of 1817, and its dimensions carefully ascertained, although from frequent plowing its form had become almost destroyed. It is situated in the township of Kingston, upon a level plain, on the north side of Toby's Creek, about one hundred and fifty feet from its bank, and about half a mile from its confluence with the Susquehanna. From present appearances, it consisted probably of only one mound, which in height and thickness appears to have been the same on all sides, and was constructed of earth, the plain on which it stands not abounding in stone. On the outside of the rampart is an intrenchment, or ditch. When the first settlers came to Wyoming, this plain was covered with its native forest, consisting principally of oak and yellow pine, and the trees which grew in the rampart and the intrenchment are said to have been as large as those in any other part of the valley; one large oak particularly, upon being cut down, was ascertained to be *seven hundred years old.* The Indians had no tradition concerning these fortifications; neither did they appear to have any knowledge of the purposes for which they were constructed. They were, perhaps, erected about the same time with those upon the waters of the Ohio, and probably by a similar people and for similar purposes."

Directly opposite, on the eastern bank of the Susquehanna, a little above the city of Wilkes-barre, another fortification has been discovered and measured, and found to have been of precisely the same size and dimensions as that described by Mr. Chapman.

In these earthen works, and along the banks of the river up as far as Towanda, have been found human skeletons,—as many as six at one time having been washed out from old fire-places by the freshets,—large earthen vessels, and relics of various kinds. One of these earthen vessels was twelve feet in diameter, thirty-six feet in circumference, and three inches thick. It was found on the farm of a Mr. Kinney. Relics of iron instruments have also been found—which agrees with a remarkable tradition of the Shawanese Indians who emigrated from Pennsylvania to Ohio, "that the coasts were inhabited by white men who used iron instruments"

Six buttons were also discovered bearing on their faces the *mermaid*, the coat of arms of the Principality of Wales

Passing thence westward to the streams which empty into the Ohio,—the Alleghany, Monongahela, Muskingum,—and down the Ohio itself on both sides, many wonderful earthen remains have been brought to view, those circular in form being the most frequent. They show, too, that they were constructed by a people who were migrating from one part of the country to another through the pressure of enemies or the inducement of more fertile lands.

In the year 1784, Mr. John Filson published a pamphlet entitled "The Discovery, Settlement, and Present State of Kentucky," wherein, after mentioning the story of Madoc, he has these words: "This account has at different times drawn the attention of the world, but, as no vestiges of them [the Welsh] had then been found, it was concluded, perhaps too rashly, to be a fable,—at least, that no remains of the colony existed. But of late years the Western settlers have received frequent accounts of a nation at a great distance up the Missouri (a branch of the Mississippi) in manners and appearance resembling other Indians, but speaking

Welsh and retaining some ceremonies of the Christian worship; and at length this is universally believed to be fact. Captain Abraham Chaplain, a gentleman whose veracity may be entirely depended upon, assured me that in the late war, being with his company in garrison at Kaskaskia, some Indians came there, and, speaking the Welsh language, were perfectly understood, and conversed with two Welshmen in his company, and that they informed them of their situation as mentioned above." Mr. Filson then continues: "That there are remains in Kentucky which prove that the country was formerly inhabited by a nation farther advanced in the arts of life than the Indians, and that these are usually attributed to the Welsh, who are supposed formerly to have inhabited these parts, that a great number of regular intrenchments are found there, and ancient fortifications with ditches and bastions,—one in particular containing about six acres of land, and others three acres; that pieces of earthenware were plowed up, a manufacture the Indians were never acquainted with."

About the time Mr. Filson's pamphlet appeared, Rev. Mr. Rankin, a resident of Kentucky, told William Owen, of London, that it was certain that a tribe or tribes of Welsh Indians then existed far westward, and that a vast uncultivated hunting-ground intervened, through which it was dangerous to pass, because of the depredations of the wild Indians, who destroyed everything that came in their way. He declared that there were unmistakable evidences of their formerly having occupied the country about Kentucky, such as *wells dug* which remained unfilled, *the ruins of buildings*, *mill-stones*, *implements of iron*, *ornaments*, etc.

The statements of these early writers have been abundantly confirmed, respecting the existence of monumental remains and traces of civilized life, by the patient explorations of such workers as Schoolcraft, Squier, Davis, Pidgeon, and others, who have opened up many of these half-concealed monuments and disclosed their contents. Squier, in speaking of those found along the Ohio Valley, says, "The British Islands only afford works with which any comparison can safely be instituted. The 'ring-forts' of the ancient Celts are nearly identical in form and structure with a large class of remains in our own country." The same author has given some deeply interesting accounts in his "Aboriginal Monuments" of his explorations of mounds, his finding human skeletons in rude frame-works of timber, instruments and ornaments of silver, copper, stone, and bone, sculptures of the human head, pottery of various kinds, and a large number of articles, some of which evince great skill in art He says, "In every instance falling within our observation, the skeleton has been so much decayed that any attempt to restore the skull, or indeed any portion of it, was hopeless.

Considering that the earth around these skeletons is wonderfully compact and dry, and that the conditions for their preservation were exceedingly favorable, while in fact they are so much decayed, we may form some estimate of their remote antiquity. In the barrows and cromlechs of the ancient Britons, entire and well-preserved skeletons are found, although having an undoubted antiquity of eighteen hundred years." There is, however, no safe rule by which to judge the antiquity of human skeletons by the surroundings. Some have been kept in a wonderful state of preservation under apparently the least favorable conditions, while others have crumbled to dust when it was thought they ought to have been preserved.

It must be borne in mind that these mounds bear no resemblance to Indian burying-grounds. They are the sepulchres of a superior people.

In 1844 a gentleman in Ohio sent to the librarian of the American Antiquarian Society, Worcester, Massachusetts, a cross, the emblem of the Christian faith. It was made of silver, and was about two and a half inches long. It was found on the breast of a female skeleton which was dug from a mound at Columbus, over which a forest of trees had grown. On this cross the capital letters I. S. are perfectly visible. These initials are interpreted to mean the sacred name, Iesus Salvator.

A relic which obtained great celebrity some

years ago, and which is now in the possession of some person in Richmond, Virginia, was found at Grave Creek, Virginia, near the Ohio, in the upper vault of the celebrated mound there. The attention of the learned world was brought to it by Mr Schoolcraft, who made a correct drawing and published it. The mound went by the suggestive name of "*The Grave.*" It was pointed out to travellers on the Ohio, and was frequently visited. Dates were cut upon the trees surmounting it as early as 1734. The relic was found, with other things, by the side of some skeletons. It is nearly circular in form, and composed of a compact sandstone of a light color. The inscription upon it runs in three parallel lines, and comprises twenty-four distinct characters, having at the bottom a hieroglyphic or ideographic sign. It has been subjected to the studious scrutiny of many learned men, with various results The most of the characters have been decided to be Celtic or old British; and therefore they afford some clue as to the origin of the relic itself. The very fact of these characters being alphabetical indicates that the inscription was made by those of European origin.

What, then, is the conclusion? That it was inscribed by those who understood the old British or Welsh language, who occupied the valley of the Ohio centuries ago, and who were the followers or descendants of Madoc.

Some years ago, a circular plate, made of copper

and overlaid with a thick plate of silver on one side, was found near the city of Marietta, Ohio The copper was nearly reduced to an oxide, or rust. The silver was black, but could be brightened by being rubbed. A small piece of leather was inserted between the two plates of silver and copper, and both held together with a central rivet. This relic exactly resembled the bosses or ornaments appended to the belt of the broadsword of the ancient Briton or Welshman. It lay on the face of the skeleton, preserving the bone, as it did the leather and the lint or flax around the rivet. Near the body was found a plate of silver, six inches long and two in breadth, and weighing one ounce. There were also several pieces of a copper tube, filled with rust

These are supposed to have belonged to the equipage of a sword; though nothing but iron rust could be found to answer for such a weapon. Near the feet of the skeleton was a copper plumb, of about three ounces' weight, and resembling an ordinary clock-weight.

The construction of the earthen defences found in the valley of the Ohio and along the Mississippi evinces that those who erected them had great proficiency in engineering and military skill. They comprised all the parts of a systematic defence,—walls, ramparts, fosses, intrenchments, and even the lookout, corresponding to the *barbican* in the British system of the Middle Ages. So that it may be asked, in the language of Dr. S. P. Hildreth, a zealous antiquarian of Marietta, Ohio, "Of what age, or of what nation, was this race that once inhabited the territory drained by the Ohio? From what we see of their works, they must have been acquainted with some of the fine arts and sciences. They have left us perfect specimens of circles, squares, octagons, parallel lines, on a grand and noble scale; and, unless it can be proved that they had intercourse with Asia or Europe, we must attribute to them the art of working metals."

But the red race knew nothing of the art or science of smelting raw ores. Their copper instruments were beaten into shape from the native metal, and these at best were very rare and rude. The hundreds and thousands of relics in the various metals, many curiously finished, found in the valleys of the Ohio and Mississippi, in mounds and caves, must, therefore, be the product of another people. Nor is it necessary to go back to dim or immemorial ages to account for their origin.

The Welsh are the best miners and workers in metals in the world. The Phœnicians carried on a large trade in the metals with the inhabitants of the British Isles centuries before the Christian era, and their mines of iron, copper, tin, etc., have since enriched the British Empire.

The mines of the Upper Lake regions were doubtless worked by the Welsh in the thirteenth, fourteenth, and fifteenth centuries, all the evidences seeming to allow four or five hundred years since their opening. Old trees showing three hundred and ninety-five rings of annual growth have been found standing among the débris at the surface of some of these mines. Huge chunks of copper, in some cases weighing six tons, have been lifted out of their beds by finished tools and mining appliances.

Wooden frame-works and skids have been found, which were made with sharp-edged instruments, but upon being exposed to the air have turned to dust. It is thought that the area covered by the ancient works in the Lake Superior region is more extensive than that which includes the modern mines, but that the forests have overgrown and conceal from view the excavations. Of course a considerable period elapsed after the Welsh occupied the Ohio valley before they and those with whom they became incorporated penetrated so far northward to work these mines. Most of the relics which have been discovered in the mounds were, in all probability, made from the metals of that region. Colonel Whittlesey, who is an authority on this subject, thinks that the miners "went up from the settlements farther south in the summers, remained in the copper regions through the season, and worked the mines in organized companies until the advance of winter terminated their operations. As they were more advanced in civilization than the aborigines, they probably had better means of transportation than bark canoes."

In the enthusiasm of antiquarian research, many have been led to assign too great an age to the earthen defences and mounds of our country. The Cardiff Giant was pronounced, with scholarly awe, to be a fine specimen of an extinct race which trod this earth thousands of years before Adam drew breath, but was subsequently discovered to have been made from a chunk of gypsum taken from a quarry in Iowa The remains of Fort Necessity, erected to cover the retreat of Braddock's defeated army, now wear such an antiquarian aspect that if there were no historical data respecting them they would be classed with the mounds. So with Forts Hamilton and Meigs, on the Miami and Maumee Rivers, and others, constructed only about one hundred years ago. When native forest trees are cleared away and the soil is turned over for the purpose of embankments, a new growth of vegetation is quickly started.

Some years ago, a large oak was cut down in Lyons, New York, and on its being sawed there were found near the centre the marks of an axe. On counting the concentric circles, it was discovered that four hundred and sixty had been formed since the cutting was made. The block was brought to Newark and exhibited in a hotel there. All who saw it declared that the work had been done with an *edged* tool.

The trees covering the mounds in Wyoming, as

described by Chapman, had annular rings numbering from six to seven hundred. President Harrison observed that it would take the trees, growing where a forest was cut down fifty years since, five hundred years to equal in height the surrounding woods; and that a forest of the largest trees at the mouth of the Great Miami, consisting of fifteen acres, covers the ruins left by former races.

It is worthy of notice, too, that the age of the trees found standing on these ancient fortifications and mounds, and the number of their annular circles, diminish with striking regularity in the ratio of their distance from the eastern coast. The first found reach as high a number as seven hundred; then, decreasing, they are found in Ohio with from four hundred to five hundred; and then in the copper regions of Lake Superior with from three hundred and fifty to four hundred annular rings. Comparing these figures with the time (1170) when Madoc and his followers landed on this continent, and allowing for their progress into the interior such reasonable periods as their peculiar circumstances demanded, adding also whatever other proofs have been adduced, scarcely a single doubt can linger in the mind of the candid inquirer as to the origin of these earthen defences and mounds, the removal of the native forests, the working of the mines, and the many relics unearthed.

If it be objected that a small band of a few

hundreds could not cover so much territory or accomplish so much work, it may be said, in reply, that one century alone offers sufficient time for the achievement of wonders. Under favorable conditions peoples multiply rapidly. Surrounded as the Welsh were with populous tribes of red men, they affiliated with some of them for self-protection and aid, and degraded remnants of them are found at the present time in different parts of the far West.

CHAPTER VIII.

THE DISPERSION OF THE WELSH INDIANS.

It was only after the most stubborn and sanguinary resistance that the Welsh Indians yielded the fertile plains of the Ohio valley to their enemies. They moved down the Ohio River to its confluence with the Mississippi, and here for a period took another stand, as is evinced by the many remarkable remains and relics which have been brought to light by accident and the diligent researches of antiquarians and archæologists.

At this point there began a series of dispersions, south, west, and north, by which they became spread over a vast area of the Western country. The Lower and Upper Mississippi, the Missouri, and many of the smaller rivers abound with remains which exhibit the same knowledge and skill with those along the Ohio. Such a dispersion offers the best solution for the construction of the numerous accounts given of them into an intelligible and consistent whole. These accounts coming from so many different parties, separated from one another in time and distance, and independent of one another, excluding the possibility of preconcert or collusion, it would not be wonderful if they appeared to vary in the minor details. Their differences are a proof of the absence of falsehood or trickery. That the Welsh did not lose all the radical characteristics of their race can be made evident: still, when it is considered how numerous the peoples were with whom they amalgamated, it will be seen that it did not require a great length of time for them to exhibit also traits of savage life. Such a result would follow from physical laws and the conditions of their wild state

This dispersion, and their being discovered in various sections of the country along and west of the Mississippi, will account for the different names by which they were called by intelligent travellers and captured whites, who had either heard of them or had been in their country and conversed with them.

In 1792 a gentleman who had resided more than twenty years in New Orleans and on the banks of the Mississippi wrote a letter to Griffith Williams, London, being on a visit to the latter city himself at the time, from which the following extract is given: "That the natives of America have, for many years past, emigrated from the east to the west is a known fact. That the tribes mentioned by Mr. Jones, who spoke the Welsh tongue, may have done so is much within the order of probability; and that a people called the Welsh or White Indians now reside at or near the banks of the Missouri, I have not the least doubt of, having been so often assured of it by people who have traded in that river, and who could have no possible inducement to relate such a story unless it had been founded in fact.

"Since writing the above, a merchant from the Illinois country, and a person of reputation, is arrived in London. He assures me there is not the smallest doubt of a people existing on the west side of the Mississippi, called by the French the White Bearded Indians, none of the natives of America wearing beards; that these people are really white; that they are said to consist of thirty-two villages or towns, are exceeding civilized, and vastly attached to certain religious ceremonies; that a Mr. Ch , a merchant of reputation at the Illinois, has been to their country, which is, as he supposes, upwards of a thousand miles from the Illinois.

"Yours, etc ,

"J. J."

Mr. Williams, to whom the above was written, adds, "I have met the above gentleman several times, and he confirms the latter part of this narrative; that Mr. Ch. is a near relation of his; that Mr. Ch. was introduced to the chief of the Padoucas, by whom he was received with much solemnity, owing to his being of white complexion, from which circumstance, as far as Mr. Ch could understand by being amongst them, he was deemed an angel of God, his hands and his feet being washed by order of the chief, who appeared much advanced in years, his hair being long and perfectly white; that the people chiefly subsist by the produce of the chase; that the instruments they use on the occasion are generally bows and arrows; that the farther he advanced from the frontiers, the different tribes he passed through were the more civilized."

Upon the occasion of the visit of General Bowles, a chief of the Cherokees, to London, on official business, in 1792, he was waited on by several eminent Welsh gentlemen to inquire if he knew anything of the Welsh Indians. He replied, "Yes, I know them, and they are called the Padoucas, or White Indians. This title is given them because of their complexions." When a map was laid before him on which that name was inscribed, he said that these were the people, and showed the limits of their country. He said that "generally they were called the White Padoucas, but those who live in the northern parts are called Black Padoucas, because they are a mixture of the White Padoucas and other Indians. The White Padoucas are as you are, having some of them sandy, some red, and some black hair They are very numerous, and one of the most warlike people on the continent."

The gentlemen present then informed General Bowles of the times and circumstances of Madoc's voyages, when he replied, "They must have been as early as that period, otherwise they could not have increased to be so numerous a people. I have travelled their southern boundaries from one side to the other, but have never entered their country. Another reason I have for thinking them to be Welsh is, that a Welshman was with me at home for some time, who had been a prisoner among the Spaniards and had worked in the mines of Mexico, and by some means he contrived to escape, got into the wilds, and made his way across the continent, and eventually passed through the midst of the Padoucas, and at once found himself with a people with whom he could converse, and he stayed for some time. He told me that they had several books, which were most religiously preserved in skins and were considered by them as mysteries. These they believed gave an account from whence they came. They said they had not seen a white man like themselves, who was a stranger, for a long time."

General Bowles was of Irish descent, and had many respectable relatives residing in London, whither he had come on a public mission in behalf of the Cherokees.

Mr. Price, another chief, who was born among the Creeks, said that he understood not the Welsh tongue, but that his father, who was a Welshman, had frequent interviews and conversed with the Padoucas in his native language. He lived the greatest part of his life in the Creek country, and died there.

In Cox's description of Louisiana, 1782, p. 63, it is said "that Baron La Hontan, having traced the Missouri for eight hundred miles due west, found an east lake, along which resided two or three great nations, much more civilized than other Indians; and that out of this lake a great river disembogues itself into the South Sea."

The name by which he designates these people is Metocantes.

Charlevoix, vol. ii. p. 225 of the English translation, mentions "a great lake very far to the west of the Mississippi, on the banks of which are a peoble resembling the French, with buttons on their clothes, living in cities, and using horses in hunting buffaloes; that they are clothed with the skins of that animal, but without any arms but the bow and arrow." He calls them the Mactotatas.

Bossu, in his account of Louisiana, vol. i. p 182, says that he had been informed by the Indians of a nation of clothed people, far to the westward of the Mississippi, who inhabited great villages built with white stone, navigated in great piraguas on the great salt-water lakes, and were governed by one despotic chief, who sent great armies into the field.

On page 393 he gives a particular account of Madoc's alleged voyages, and observes, "The English believe that this prince discovered Virginia.

Peter Martyr seems to give a proof of it when he says that the nations of Virginia and Guatemala celebrate the memory of one of their ancient heroes, whom they call Madoc. Several modern travellers have found ancient British words used by the North American nations. The celebrated Bishop Nicholson believes that the Welsh language has formed a considerable part of the languages of the American nations. There are antiquarians who pretend that the Spaniards got their double or guttural *l* (*ll*) from the Americans, who, according to the English, must have got it from the Welsh."

Bossu adds that these Welsh Indians seem to go by various names, such as Panes, Panis (Pawnees).

During the war of the Revolution, Sir John Caldwell, Bart, was stationed on the east side of the Mississippi. He lived in the country a long time, acquired a perfect knowledge of the language of the inhabitants, was adopted by them, and married a daughter of one of their chiefs. He was informed by them that the Panis (Pawnees) were a people considerably civilized, that they cultivated the ground, and built houses. Some Welshmen in his company understood their language, which they said was Welsh. Sir John said that he became acquainted with a Mr. Pond, a very sensible and intelligent Indian trader, who frequented the country of the Panis, which lies about the head of the river Osages. He said that they were whiter and more civilized than any other Indian tribe.

Mr. Rimington said that he had known for a long time that there were civilized Indians west of the Mississippi, who were called by those on the eastern side (the Chickasaws, etc) Ka Anzou or Ka Anjou (Kansas), which in their language signifies *first of men*, or *first men*, and he was very strongly inclined to think that they were the Welsh Indians.

Mr. Rimington, who was a native of England, had been a long time among the Indians. He said that being once with several Englishmen and one Jack Hughes, a Welshman, at the Forks of the Ohio, where was an Indian mart, some strange Indians came there from the west of the Mississippi. A Shawanese Indian, who understood English, came to Mr. Rimington and desired him to be his interpreter. He went, but found that the language of these strangers was not intelligible to him. When he returned, and told his companions that he knew not their language, one of them exclaimed, "Oh, they are the Welsh Indians!" Jack Hughes was sent, who understood them well; and he was their interpreter while they continued there. He said that these Indians are tolerably white in complexion, and their dress like that of the Europeans, —a kind of trousers, coats with sleeves, and hats or caps made of small and very beautiful feathers curiously wrought. Furthermore he said that these white Indians are to be met with at the Indian marts on the Mississippi, at the Natches, Forks of the Ohio, Kaskaskies, etc, for all the Indian tribes on this continent, even from the shores of the South Sea, resort thither.

Thus it may be seen that the Welsh Indians went by different names, the most of them bearing a similitude to what they called themselves, and by which they were known to the Indians and the whites. as Padoucas by Mr. Binon, General Bowles, Mr. Ch., Mr. Price and his father; Panis (Pawnees) by Sir John Caldwell, Mr Pond, and others; Ka Anzou (Kansas) by the Chickasaws, and Mr. Rimington; Matocantes by Coxe; Mactotatas by Charlevoix; and Madawgwys, Madogian or Madogiaint by many others

Padoucas would more nearly approach the general name in sound if the letter *m* were substituted for *p*, thus changing the word into Madoucas, the former being regarded as a corruption which might arise from the difficulty some tribes have experienced in pronouncing certain letters.

In the common maps of the country a century ago, an extensive nation called the White Padoucas were placed about eighty-eight degrees north latitude, and one hundred and two degrees west longitude of London; but they extended in detached communities from about thirty-seven degrees north latitude and ninety-seven degrees west longitude to forty-three degrees north latitude and one hundred and ten degrees west longitude. The city of Paducah, Kentucky, doubtless derived its name from this nation, which once occupied the region in which it is situated. The Padoucas, Pawnees, and Kansas were intermixed with one another, and suffered a fearful decimation by wars and diseases, so that the tribal name of the first is now extinct; but a few straggling bands still survive under the second and third names. In 1874 the Pawnees numbered about two thousand eight hundred and thirty-one, and the Kansas or Kaws less than that number. From the document accompanying President Jefferson's message to Congress in 1806, it may be discovered that the Pania Pique in Arkansas were formerly known by the name of the White Panias, and are of the same family as the Panias of the river Platte. According to that communication, the Padoucas, a once powerful nation, had apparently disappeared. In 1724 they resided in villages at the head of the Kansas River. Oppressed by the Missourians, they removed to the upper part of the river Platte, where they had but little intercourse with the whites. The northern branch of that river is still called the Padoucas Fork. It is conjectured that, being still more oppressed, they divided into small wandering bands, which assumed the names of the subdivisions of the Padoucas nation which have since been known under the appellation of Wetepahatoes, Kiawas, Kanenavish, Katteka, and Dotamie, who still inhabit the country to which the Padoucas are said to have removed.

In the map attached to Du Pratz's Louisiana the "White Panis" are placed at the head of the Arkansas; Panis Mahas, or White Panis, at the head of the south branch of the Missouri; and between those rivers is marked the country of the Padoucas.

During the last two centuries the Indian races have waned so rapidly, their places of habitation have been so often changed, and so many of the tribes have become amalgamated, that names are not an unerring guide by which to determine their early history, or to what stock many of the remnants still surviving belong.

As to the names given by the French travellers cited elsewhere,—Matocantes, etc.,—there is some resemblance to the name of Madoc. A Welshwoman in South Wales calling her son by that name would say Matoc, which is pure Silurian Welsh, the *d* being changed into *t:* hence there might follow such names as Matociait, Matociaint, Matocantes, as applied to the followers of Madoc. These changes are not arbitrary, but inhere in the laws and euphony of human language.

CHAPTER IX.

MAURICE GRIFFITH'S AND HIS COMPANIONS' EXPERIENCE.

THE following letter, published in the "Kentucky Palladium" in 1804, by Judge Toulmin, of Mississippi, will be read with keen interest by those who have any desire to study everything relating to this subject:

"SIR,—No circumstance relating to the history of the Western country probably has excited, at different times, more general attention and anxious curiosity than the opinion that a nation of white men speaking the Welsh language reside high up the Missouri. By some the idea is treated as nothing but the suggestion of bold imposture and easy credulity; whilst others regard it as a fact fully authenticated by Indian testimony, and the report of various travellers worthy of credit.

* * * * * * * *

"Could the fact be well established, it would afford perhaps the most satisfactory solution of the difficulty occasioned by a view of the various ancient fortifications with which the Ohio country abounds, of any that has been offered Those fortifications were evidently never made by the Indians. The Indian art of war presents nothing of the kind. The probability, too, is that the persons who constructed them were, *at that time*, acquainted with the use of iron. The situation of these fortifications, which are uniformly in the most fertile land of the country, indicates that those who made them were an agricultural people; and the remarkable care and skill with which they were executed afford traits of the genius of a people who relied more on their military skill than on their numbers. The growth of the trees upon them is very compatible with the idea that it is not more than three hundred years ago that they were abandoned.

"These hints, however, are thrown out rather to excite inquiry than by way of advancing any decided opinion on the subject. Having never met with any of the persons who had seen these white Americans, nor even received their testimony near the source, I have always entertained considerable doubts about the fact.

"Last evening, however, Mr. John Childs, of Jessamine County, a gentleman with whom I have been long acquainted, and who is well known to be a man of veracity, communicated a relation to me which at all events appears to merit serious attention. After he had related it in conversation, I requested him to repeat it, and committed it to writing. It has certainly some internal marks of authenticity. The country described was altogether unknown in Virginia when the relation was given, and probably very little known to the Shawanese Indians. Yet the account of it agrees very remarkably with later discoveries. On the other hand, the story of the large animal, though by no means incredible, has something of the air of fable, and it does not satisfactorily appear how the long period which the party were absent was spent,—though the Indians are, however, so much accustomed to loiter away their time that many weeks, and even months, may probably have been spent in indolent repose. Without detaining you any more with preliminary remarks, I will proceed to the narration as I received it from Mr. Childs.

"Maurice Griffiths, a native of Wales, which country he left when he was about sixteen years of age, was taken prisoner by a party of Shawanese Indians, about forty years ago, near Vosses Fort, on the head of the Roanoke River, in Virginia, and carried to the Shawanese Nation. Having stayed there about two years and a half, he found that five young men of the tribe had a desire of attempting to explore the sources of the Missouri He prevailed upon them to admit him as one of their party. They set out with six good rifles and with six pounds of powder apiece, of which they were, of course, very careful.

"On reaching the mouth of the Missouri, they were struck with the extraordinary appearance occasioned by the intermixture of the muddy waters of the Missouri and the clear, transparent element of the Mississippi. They stayed there two or three days, amusing themselves with the view of this novel sight, they then determined on the course which they should pursue, which happened to be so nearly in the course of the river that they frequently came within sight of it as they proceeded on their journey. After travelling about thirty days through pretty farming woodland, they came into fine open prairies, on which nothing grew but long luxuriant grass. Here was a succession of these, varying in size, some being eight or ten miles across, but one of them was so long that it occupied three days to travel through it. In passing through this large prairie, they were much distressed for water and provisions, for they saw neither beast nor bird; and, though there was an abundance of salt springs, fresh water was very scarce. In one of these prairies the salt springs ran into small ponds, in which, as the weather was hot, the water had sunk and left the edges of the pond so covered with salt that they fully supplied themselves with that article, and might easily have collected bushels of it.

"As they were travelling through the prairies, they had likewise the good fortune to kill an animal which was nine or ten feet high and a bulk proportioned to its height. They had seen two of the same species before, and they saw four of them afterwards. They were swift-footed, and had neither tusks nor horns. After passing through the long prairie, they made it a rule never to enter on one which they could not see across, till they had supplied themselves with a sufficiency of jerked venison to last several days. After having travelled a considerable time through the prairies, they came to very extensive lead-mines, where they melted the ore and furnished themselves with what lead they wanted. They afterwards came to two copper-mines, one of which was three miles through, and in several places they met with rocks of copper ore as large as houses.

"When about fifteen days' journey from the second copper-mine, they came in sight of white mountains, which, though it was in the heat of summer, appeared to them to be covered with snow. The sight naturally excited considerable astonishment; but, on their approaching the mountains, they discovered that, instead of snow, they were covered with immense bodies of white sand.

"They had in the mean time passed through about ten nations of Indians, from whom they received very friendly treatment. It was the practice of the party to exercise the office of spokesman in rotation; and when the language of any nation through which they passed was unknown to them, it was the duty of the spokesman, a duty in which the others never interfered, to convey their meaning by appropriate signs.

"The labor of travelling through the deep sands was excessive; but at length they relieved themselves of this difficulty by following the course of a shallow river, the bottom of which being level, they made their way to the top of the mountains with tolerable convenience. After passing the mountains they entered a fine fertile tract of land, which having travelled through for several days, they accidentally *met with three white men in the Indian dress.* Griffith immediately understood their language, as it was pure Welsh, though they occasionally made use of a few words with which he was not acquainted. However, as it happened to be the turn of one of his Shawanese companions to act as spokesman or interpreter, he preserved a profound silence, and never gave them any intimation that he understood the language of their new companions.

"After proceeding with them four or five days' journey, they came to the village of these white men, where they found that the *whole nation was of the same color*, having all the European complexion. The three men took them through their villages for about the space of fifteen miles, when they came to the council-house, at which an assembly of the king and chief men of the nation was immediately held. The council lasted three days, and, as the strangers were not supposed to be acquainted with their language, they were suffered to be present at their deliberations

"The great question before the council was, what conduct should be observed towards the strangers. From their fire-arms, their knives, and their tomahawks, it was concluded that they were a warlike people. It was conceived that they were sent to look out for a country for their nation; that if they were suffered to return, they might expect a body of powerful invaders; but that if these six men were put to death, nothing would be known of their country, and they would still enjoy their possessions in security. It was finally determined that they should be put to death.

"Griffith then thought it was time for him to speak. *He addressed the council in the Welsh language.* He informed them that they had not been sent by any nation; that they were actuated merely by private curiosity, and had no hostile intentions; that it was their wish to trace the Missouri to its source; and that they should return to their country satisfied with the discoveries they had made, without any wish to disturb the repose of their new acquaintances.

"An instant astonishment glowed in the countenances, not only of the council, but of his Shawanese companions, who clearly saw that he was understood by the people of the country. Full confidence was at once given to his declarations.

The king advanced and gave him his hand. They abandoned the design of putting him and his companions to death, and from that moment treated him with the utmost friendship. Griffith and the Shawanese continued eight months in the nation, but were deterred from prosecuting their researches up the Missouri by the advice of the people of the country, who informed them that they had gone a twelvemonth's journey up the river, but found it as large there as it was in their own country.

"As to the history of this people he could learn nothing satisfactory. The only account they could give was, that their forefathers had come up the river from a very distant country. They had no books, no records, no writings. They intermixed with no other people by marriage: there was not a dark-skinned man in the nation. Their numbers were very considerable. There was a continued range of settlements on the river for fifty miles, and there were within this space three large water-courses which fell into the Missouri, on the banks of each of which they were likewise settled. He supposed that there must be fifty thousand men in the nation capable of bearing arms. Their clothing was skins well dressed. Their houses were made of upright posts and barks of trees. The only implements they had to cut them with were stone tomahawks; they had no iron Their arms were bows and arrows. They had some silver which had been hammered with stones into coarse ornaments, but it did not appear to be pure. They had neither horses, cattle, sheep, hogs, nor any domestic or tame animals. They lived by hunting. He said nothing about their religion.

"Griffith and his companions had some large iron tomahawks with them With these they cut down a tree and prepared a canoe to return home in; but their tomahawks were so great a curiosity, and the people of the country were so eager to handle them, that their canoe was completed with very little labor to them. When this work was accomplished, they proposed to leave their new friends, Griffith, however, having promised to visit them again.

"They descended the river with considerable speed, but amidst frequent dangers from the rapidity of the current, particularly when passing through the white mountains. When they reached the Shawanese Nation, they had been absent about two years and a half. Griffith supposed that when they travelled they went at the rate of about fifteen miles per day. He stayed but a few months with the Indians after his return, as a favorable opportunity offered itself to him to reach his friends in Virginia. He came with a hunting-party of Indians to the head-waters of Coal River, which runs into New River not far above the falls. Here he left the Shawanese, and easily reached the settlements on the Roanoke.

"Mr. Childs knew him before he was taken prisoner, and saw him a few days after his return, when he narrated to him the preceding circumstances. Griffith was universally regarded as a steady, honest man, and a man of strict veracity. Mr. Childs has always placed the utmost confidence in his account of himself and his travels, and has no more doubt of the truth of his relations than if he had seen the whole himself. Whether Griffith be still alive or not he does not know. Whether his ideas be correct or not, we shall probably have a better opportunity of judging on the return of Captains Lewis and Clarke, who, though they may not penetrate as far as Griffith alleged he had done, will probably learn enough of the country to enable us to determine whether the account given by Griffith be fiction or truth.

"I am, sir,

"Your humble servant,

"HARRY TOULMIN.

"FRANKFORT, December 12, 1804"

With regard to the exploring expeditions of Lewis and Clarke, to which Judge Toulmin refers, it was found in their published records that although they pursued a different branch of the Missouri from the one which was supposed to lead to the Welsh Indians, they discovered straggling Indians similar to those mentioned by Griffith, Vancouver, and many others. They belonged to those who had a tribal existence in other localities.

However, they describe long lines of embankments which they saw before leaving the main channel of the Missouri, some of them enclosing an area of six hundred acres. They found them as high up as one thousand miles from the junction with the Mississippi. Captain Lewis was a Welshman. In their long and perilous journey, extending to the Columbia River, they lost but one man, William Floyd, also a Welshman, and who was buried on top of one of these mounds west of the Missouri,—called to this day "*Floyd's Mound*"

The Missouri, taken in connection with the Mississippi, is the longest river in the world, its length from the highest navigable stream to the Gulf of Mexico being four thousand four hundred and ninety-one miles, and its length to its junction with the Mississippi, three thousand and ninety-six miles. Add to this the immense distance not navigable because of the cataracts and falls, next to Niagara the grandest on this globe, and reaching to the Rocky Mountains, and some idea may be formed of the great extent of this river. The entrance of the Yellow-Stone is nearly two thousand miles above its mouth. A journey of one thousand miles up the Missouri a century or more since, while it was an undertaking of no slight magnitude and attended with many hardships and dangers, did not bring the traveller over more than one-fourth of its length. The course pursued by Griffith and his companions can be marked out with singular accuracy by the use of subsequent knowledge, obtained during the last one hundred years, respecting the country that river traverses.

He speaks of finding lead mines. The lead-mines of Missouri are extremely valuable, and yield millions of pounds annually.

He speaks of salt springs The line of his journey conducted him by the salt licks of Nebraska, which, when the springs are low and evaporation is rapid, have the appearance of layers of snow.

He speaks of white mountains. Passing from the broad open prairies to the uplands and mountains, the soil is sandy and in many places remarkably white. The writer himself has often seen on the Missouri bold projections of limestone which in the distance appeared like banks of snow.

He speaks of the Indians being all white. This presents a difficulty not easily reconcilable with the intermixture theory. The predominating color, it would be supposed, was that of the red race. But he partially explains this by saying that "they intermixed with no other people by marriage: there was not a dark-skinned man in the nation." Could they without intermixture have increased to such considerable numbers as to be able, as he supposes, to put into the field "fifty thousand men capable of bearing arms"? It need not be thought impossible, but it certainly is improbable. At any rate, this people were sufficiently white to be called, by Griffith and by a large number of reliable witnesses, "White Padoucas," "White Panis," "White Indians."

He speaks of their having no records and no horses. In this respect his recital differs somewhat from those given by others, some of whom assert that they saw some old manuscript books, and that they had horses for the chase. His statement, however, offers no contradiction to that made by others, because it is pretty certain that many of them came upon different branches of the same extensive nation.

He speaks of their speaking "pure Welsh," but qualifies it by saying that they occasionally made use of a few words with which he was not acquainted. He meant no more than that the radical structure of the language was still preserved and could be readily distinguished, though some of the words had undergone modification. This is the case with all languages, not even excepting the Welsh in Wales, which has shown itself superior to all others to resist any great change.

It is somewhat surprising that Griffith did not give some account of the religious institutions of this people; for if they were the descendants of Madoc some traces of the Christian religion might have been discovered. Or had they been all effaced in six hundred years?

It must be admitted that what he does relate bears every internal mark of simple, honest truth.

CHAPTER X.

CAPTAIN ISAAC STUART—GOVERNORS SEVIER AND DINWIDDIE—GENERAL MORGAN LEWIS—THEIR KNOWLEDGE OF THE WELSH INDIANS.

CAPTAIN STUART was an officer in the Provincial Cavalry of South Carolina, and the following sketch was taken from his own lips by I. C., Esq., an intelligent gentleman, in March, 1782. Lieutenant-Colonel Conger, of South Carolina, regarded Captain Stuart as a man who could be implicitly trusted in what he said.

"I was taken prisoner about fifty miles to the westward of Fort Pitt, about eighteen years ago, by the Indians, and was carried by them to the Wabash, with many more white men, who were executed with circumstances of horrid barbarity. It was my good fortune to call forth the sympathy of what is called the good woman of the town, who was permitted to redeem me from the flames by giving as my ransom a horse.

"After remaining two years in bondage among the Indians, a Spaniard came to the nation, having been sent from Mexico on discoveries. He made application to the chief for redeeming me and another white man, who was in like situation, named John Davey (David), which they complied with.

"And we took our departure, in company with the Spaniard, to the westward, crossing the Mississippi near Rouge, or Red, River, up which we travelled seven hundred miles, when we came to a nation remarkably white, and whose hair was of a reddish color, or mostly so. They lived on the banks of a small river which is called the river Post. In the morning of the day after our arrival, the Welshman informed me that he was determined to remain with them, giving as a reason that he understood their language, it being very little different from the Welsh. My curiosity was excited very much by this information, and I went with my companion to the chief men of the town, who informed him, in a language I had no knowledge of, and which had no affinity to that of other Indian tongues that I ever heard, that their forefathers of this nation came from a foreign country and landed on the east side of the Mississippi, describing the country particularly now called Florida, and that on the Spaniards taking possession of Mexico they fled to their then abode.

"And, as a proof of the truth of what he advanced, he brought forth *a roll of parchment*, which was carefully tied up in otters' skins, on which were large characters written with blue ink. The characters I did not understand; and, the Welshman being unacquainted with letters, even of his own language, I was not able to know the meaning of the writing. They are a bold, hardy, and intrepid people, very warlike, and the women beautiful when compared with other Indians."

John Sevier, at one time Governor of Tennessee, in a letter dated October 9, 1810, and published by Major Stoddard in his "Sketches, Historical and Descriptive, of Louisiana," Philadelphia, 1812, p. 483, says that in 1782 he was on a campaign against the Cherokees. Observing on his route traces of very ancient fortifications, he afterwards took occasion, on exchange of prisoners, to inquire into their origin, of Oconostoto, who for sixty years had been a ruling chief of the Cherokee Nation, and particularly as to the origin of the remarkable fortifications on the branch of the Highwasse River. The venerable chief replied, that it was handed down by their forefathers that those works were made by *white people* who had formerly inhabited the country. When the Cherokees lived in the country now South Carolina, wars existed between them, and were only ended when the whites consented to abandon the country. Accordingly, they ascended the Tennessee to the Ohio, then to the big river Mississippi, then up the muddy Missouri to a very great distance. They are now on some of its branches, but are no longer white people; they have become Indians, and look somewhat like the other red people of the country. "I then asked him," continues Governor Sevier, "if he had ever heard any of his ancestors say to what nation of people the whites belonged. He answered, 'I heard my grandfather and other old people say that they were a people called Welsh; that they had crossed the great waters and landed near the mouth of the Alabama River, and were finally driven to the heads of its waters, and even to the Highwasse River, by the Mexican Spaniards.'

"Oconostoto also said that an old woman in his nation had some parts of an old book given her by an Indian living high up the Missouri, and thought he was one of the Welsh tribe. Unfortunately," observes Governor Sevier, "before I had an opportunity of seeing the book, her house and all its contents were destroyed by fire. I have conversed with several persons who saw and examined it; but it was so worn and disfigured that nothing intelligible remained."

Governor Sevier was informed by a Frenchman, a great explorer of the country west of the Mississippi, that he had been high up the Missouri, and traded several months with the Welsh tribes, who spoke much of the Welsh dialect. Although their customs were savage and wild, yet many of them, particularly the females, were fair and white. They often told him that they had sprung from a white people; and that they had yet some small scraps of books remaining, but in such a tattered and mutilated order that they were unintelligible

The very year that Robert Dinwiddie, Governor

of Virginia, sent a letter of remonstrance to M de St. Pierre, the French commander, complaining of the hostile movements of The Ohio Company, George Washington, then a young man of twenty-two, being chosen bearer of the dispatches, the Governor received a letter from a gentleman named George Chrochan, showing that the French knew of the Welsh Indians. This was in 1753. The original letter was deposited in the Foreign Office in London, and several gentlemen were enabled to obtain copies of it through Maurice Morgan, Esq., secretary to Sir Guy Carleton. It is as follows:

"Last year I understood, by Colonel Lomax, that your Honor would be glad to have some information of a nation of people settled to the west, on a large river that runs to the Pacific Ocean, *commonly called the Welsh Indians.*

"As I had an opportunity of gathering some accounts of those people, I make bold, at the instance of Colonel Cressup, to send you the following accounts. As I formerly had an opportunity of being acquainted with several French traders, and particularly with one who was bred up from his infancy amongst the Western Indians on the west side of Lake Erie, he informed me that the first intelligence the French had of them was by some Indians settled at the back of New Spain, who, in their way home, happened to lose themselves, and fell down on this settlement of people, which they took to be French by their talking very quick; so, on their return to Canada, they informed the Governor that there was a large settlement of French on a river that ran to the sun's setting; that they were not Indians, although they lived within themselves as Indians; for they could not perceive that they traded with any people, or had any trade to sea, for they had no boats or ships as they could see; and, though they had guns amongst them, yet they were so old and so much out of order that they made no use of them, but hunted with their bows and arrows for the support of their families.

"On this account the Governor of Canada determined to send a party to discover whether they were French or not, and had three hundred men raised for that purpose.

"But, when they were ready to go, the Indians would not go with them, but told the Governor if he sent but a few men they would go and show them the country; on which the Governor sent three young priests, who dressed themselves in Indian dresses and went with those Indians to the place where these people were settled, and found them to be Welsh

"They brought some old Welsh Bibles, to satisfy the Governor that they were there; and they told him that these people had a great aversion to the French, for they found by them that they had been at first settled at the mouth of the Mississippi, but had been almost cut off by the French there: so that a small remnant of them escaped back to where they were then settled, but had since become a numerous people. The Governor of Canada, on this account, determined to raise an army of French Indians to go and cut them off; but, as the French have been embarrassed in war with several other nations nearer home, I believe they have laid that project aside. The man who furnished me with this account told me that the messengers who went to make this discovery were gone sixteen months before they returned to Canada: so that these people must live at a great distance from thence due west. This is the most particular account I ever could get from those people as yet.

"I am yours, etc.,
"GEORGE CHROCHAN.

"WINCHESTER, August 24, 1753"

Governor Dinwiddie became so positively assured of their existence that he agreed with a party of black traders to go in quest of the Welsh Indians, and promised to give them for that purpose the sum of five hundred pounds; but he was recalled before they could set out on the expedition.

General Morgan Lewis was an officer in the American Revolutionary army. He was the son of Francis Lewis, one of the signers of the Declaration of Independence. The general was a well-known citizen of New York. He was aide-de-camp to General Gates at the battle of Saratoga, and, on the surrender of the English army at that place, was requested by him to receive the sword of General Burgoyne. In Turnbull's picture, commemorative of the event, found in the rotunda of the Capitol at Washington, the figure of General Lewis occupies a prominent position. He was distinguished for many honorable military and civil services. He was the successor of George Clinton as Governor of the State. In 1838 he became president of the Society of Cincinnati, an institution founded by Washington, who was its first president. His portrait hangs in the Governor's room of the New York City Hall. He died on the 7th of May, 1844, in his ninetieth year, beloved and respected by all. He used frequently to relate many stirring incidents which occurred during the life of his father. The latter, while on a military expedition in the French War, was captured at Oswego, and was assigned over, with thirty others, by Montcalm, the acting French commander, to certain Indians, as their share of prisoners. Among the Indians was a chief whose language resembled the Gaelic (a dialect of the Celtic with which Mr. Lewis, who was a native of Wales, was thoroughly acquainted). On hearing him converse, Mr. Lewis understood him sufficiently to discover that his language was of that ancient dialect, although modified by usage and lapse of time. He then addressed the chief in Welsh, and was understood. The chief selected Mr. Lewis from the rest of the prisoners, and accompanied and guarded him personally. Subsequently Mr. Lewis was sent to England in a cartel for exchange of prisoners, and after his return frequently mentioned to his family and others the circumstances. His name and memory are linked with the immortal band of signers. He was a merchant of New York city, owned property on Long Island which was destroyed by the English, and died in 1803, aged ninety years, the father and the son having attained the same age.

Here are several strong testimonies from four entirely independent sources, each separate from the others, with no motives of prejudice or self-interest to mislead wilfully, and the parties too intelligent to be betrayed into a blind credulity. The disclosures of this chapter, if they stood alone, would be sufficient to carry conviction to every candid inquirer, that there was a remarkable people, different from the common red races of this continent, inhabiting a portion of the Western country during the last century. And to such an extent did this conviction prevail that it was made the basis of official action by Governor Dinwiddie, whose plans were frustrated by his recall, and the Governor of Canada, who sent out an expedition, which returned in safety and reported the existence of Welsh Indians.

Mr. Binon, Captain Stuart, Governor Sevier, the members of the Canadian expedition, and others, state that these people had manuscript books in parchment, but that they could not be read or understood even by those Welshmen who were with some of these parties. Some of these manuscripts contained the mysteries of religion, and were carefully preserved.

Even to this day there are classes of the population of Wales who cannot read and write; a century ago their condition was far worse, before the establishment of parish schools; but, granting that all were learned in the rudiments of education, there is not probably one in a thousand who could read a manuscript of the twelfth century. Most of them stagger those who claim to have scholarly attainments. If they were in the Greek instead of the Roman character, as some of them have been discovered to be, the mystery would be still greater. The Greek alphabetical character was used in the British Island prior to the invasion by Julius Cæsar, after which the Roman character was adopted and became generally used in common life and writing.

Yet so sacred was the Greek character held by monastic schools, because the gospel was written in it, that many transcribers—and they were the book-makers—clung with a religious enthusiasm to it. Christianity was certainly introduced into the Island in the second century, the Greek forms in the Welsh language had not become lost, and it is likely that many parchment manuscripts were extant. Madoc's position as a member of the royal house of Wales, notwithstanding the scarcity and great cost of books in those times, would enable him to possess some of the most valuable, even those illuminated in rich, fixed colors, and which required many years of patient toil to manufacture It is far more within the order of reason to believe that Madoc and his emigrants, upon leaving their own native shores, would take with them copies of the great book of books,—the king of books on the throne of letters,—than that they would leave them behind. Some of his followers, perhaps the most of them, were not able to read them then, but knew somewhat their contents. Under their new conditions of life, relapsing gradually from a civilized state, these manuscripts came at length to be invested with a certain sacred mystery, as the depository of their ancestors' religious faith. No wonder that they should be so carefully preserved.

CHAPTER XI.

THE MANDAN INDIANS: WHO ARE THEY?

During the present century various travellers have called the attention of the civilized world to a small body of Indians inhabiting the banks of the Upper Missouri, called Mandans. They, with the Minatarees and Crows, are classed with the Dacotahs or Sioux, although it is known that their language bears no affinity whatever with the latter people. The Mandans are very light-colored.

George Catlin, the well-known student of Indian life, character, language, and manners, was, without any doubt, more intimately acquainted with this people than any others who preceded him or have followed him.

Mr. Catlin was born in Wyoming, Pennsylvania, and was for some years a practising lawyer. He removed to Philadelphia, and, upon meeting with a delegation of Indians, resolved to employ his talents as a painter in the best school, by painting man in the simplicity of his nature. Accordingly, he made arrangements to spend the most of his time among the Indian tribes of the Western country. His enthusiasm in his work arose to the height of an intense passion. He studied every phase of Indian life, nothing seeming to have escaped his attention. Withal, he was an ardent admirer of the Indian character; and he says, "No Indian ever struck me, betrayed me, or stole from me a shilling's worth of my property, that I am aware of." In another place he says, with a touching pathos, "They are fast travelling to the shades of their fathers, towards the setting sun." In his "Notes on the American Indians" he has portrayed a complete picture of the Mandans, giving the minutest details, so that the reader can study them as well from his two volumes as if he were daily living among them,—indeed, better than if he wished to visit them at present, they have been of late years so much reduced by the ravages of that fearful scourge, smallpox. After Mr. Catlin visited them, this disease was introduced by one of the steamers of the Fur Company, which had two cases aboard.

One reason assigned why so many perished was, that the Mandan villages were surrounded by the hostile Sioux. Many destroyed themselves with knives and guns, while others dashed their brains out against rocks, by leaping from the ledges. When the disease was at its greatest height, there was one incessant crying to the Great Spirit. The bodies lay in loathsome piles in their wigwams, and there remained to decay or be devoured by dogs. Some became crazed, and plunged into the coldest water when the fever was raging, and died before they could get out.

Mat-to-toh-pa, "Four Bears," great chief of the Mandans, watched his tribe, wives, and children die about him, then starved himself, dying on the ninth day, his body prostrate over the remains of his kinsmen. Their numbers are now so reduced that the last statistics give them four hundred only.

When Mr. Catlin made his first entrance into this nation, numbering several thousands, he was struck with their appearance, and at once concluded that they belonged to an amalgam of native and white. He was at a loss for some time how to account for this; and it was only after the most careful study that he reached the conviction that the Mandans were a branch of the descendants of Madoc's colony. He believed that the ten ships of Madoc, or at least a part of them, either entered the Balize at the mouth of the Mississippi, or the colonists landed on the Florida coast and made their way inward. They began agriculture, but were attacked and driven to erect those immense earthen fortifications, and subsequently were driven still farther and farther inward. Mandans was a corruption of Madawgwys, a name applied by Cambrians to the followers of Madoc.

The following brief summary, arranged by the writer of these pages, may be taken as Mr. Catlin's principal reasons why he thought the Mandans were Welsh:

(1) Their physical appearance.

They were of medium height, and stout. They did not share that high, stalwart physical frame which is so usual with Indians of the forest before they have become degraded by the vices of civilization.

Their complexions were very light-colored, but not uniform in shade.

Their hair was of all colors found in civilized societies. The hair of the unmixed Indian is a straight black. They wore beards,—which Indians do not have. They must have been the people who were called the Bearded Indians They had different-colored eyes,—hazel, gray, and blue.

(2.) Form of Mandan villages. Here it may be remarked that the Minatarees construct their villages upon the same plan. They sink holes in the ground to the depth of two feet and having a diameter of forty feet, of a circular form, for the foundation of their wigwams, which are built of substantial materials and display more skill than is found among the other Indians.

(3.) Mandan remains. The method of sinking down into the earth for the purpose of obtaining a foundation has, singularly enough, offered a clue as to the authors of all those remains along the Ohio, at the confluence of the Mississippi and Ohio, and along up the Missouri to the present abode of the Mandans. Their earthen works and huts, built in Druidic circles, are exact counterparts of those along the paths of their migrations. Of course the larger works have no modern counterparts, for those were erected when they were more numerous and able to cope with their foes.

The villages of the dead are uniformly built in circles.

(4) Their social and domestic customs.

They exhibit great skill in the manufacture of pottery, and the specimens found in the earthen remains of the Ohio Valley, many of them at present in the museum at Cincinnati, correspond with many of the products of the Mandans. The Mandan women mould vases, cups, pitchers, and pots out of the black clay, and bake them in little kilns in the sides of the hill, or under the bank of the river. They possess secrets of manufacturing known only to themselves. They have the extraordinary art of making a very beautiful and lasting kind of blue glass beads, which they wear on their necks in great abundance. This must be the nation, or at least a portion of it, which Captains Lewis and Clarke saw, and whom they declared to be light-colored, and whose manufacture of beads and glass articles they described thirty years before Mr Catlin.

Their canoes are the exact shape of the Welsh coracle, made of raw hides,—skins of buffaloes,—stretched underneath a frame made of willows or other boughs, and shaped nearly round like a tub, which the women carry on their heads. The

Welsh coracle, a boat which has been used by fishermen from time immemorial, is made in the same way by covering a wicker frame with leather or oil-cloth, and is carried on the head or with straps from the shoulders.

In their social and domestic habits generally they are different from other Indians.

(5.) Their religious belief and ceremonies.

There is something reaching the marvellous connected with their religion. Their traditional belief one would imagine was nothing less than a corrupted epitome of the Christian belief.

(*a.*) The account of the transgression of mother Eve, involving the doctrine of the temptation, is quite explicit. The Evil Spirit, who was a black fellow, came and sat down by a woman and told her to take a piece out of his side, which she did, and ate it, which proving to be buffalo fat, she became *enceinte.*

(*b.*) The traditions of the Deluge are far more rational, and could more easily be believed, than many which have been entertained by other nations.

(*c.*) The most important religious ceremony among the Mandans is a representation of the death and sacrifice of Jesus Christ. It takes place annually, as soon as the willow is in full leaf; for, they say, "the twig which the bird brought in was a willow bough, and had full-grown leaves upon it." The spectacle presented in the crucifixion of the Saviour by the young men of the Mandan nation might not accord with our civilized tastes and notions of propriety, yet it is wonderfully impressive, and calculated to turn the spectator's thoughts to the tragedy of Calvary. The finest-looking young man is selected as the central figure, and others surround him, when they are stuck full of skewers, and suspended on beams around their rude temple where they worship.

(6.) The Mandan language.

In their own language they call themselves See-pohs-ka-mi-mah-ka-kee (the people of the pheasants), which Mr. Catlin thinks they would not do if they had not lived where pheasants abounded, as in Pennsylvania, Ohio, and Indiana, for there are none on the prairies until within six or seven hundred miles of the Rocky Mountains.

The most convincing proof, probably, to the mind of Mr. Catlin, and to all others who have studied the possible identification of the Mandans with Madoc's colony, is found in their language. The resemblance in form and sound is so very marked that it cannot escape the eye and ear of any individual, much less those of a Welshman. It is expected that he would catch the soonest any similarity in the two languages,—the Mandan and the Welsh. And fortunately there are too many instances of this similarity to admit for a moment the idea of chance or coincidence.

That the reader may see that this is the case,

his attention is called to the subjoined table of words selected from the English, Mandan, and Welsh, and their pronunciations:

English.	Mandan	Welsh.	Pronounced.
I	Me	Mi	Me.
You	Ne	Chwi	Chwe.
He	E	A	A.
She	Ea	E	A.
It	Ount	Hwynt	Hooynt.
We	Eonah	Huna, *masc*	Hoona.
		Hona, *fem.*	Hona.
Those ones	. . . .	. . . .	Yrhai Hyna.
No, or there is not	Megosh	Nagoes	Nagosh.
No	Meg	Nage Nag Na	
Head	Pan	Pen	Pen.
The Great Spirit	Maho peneta	Mawr penaethir	Maoor penaethir.
		Ysprid mawr	Usprid maoor.
Father	Tautah	Tadwys	Tadoos
Foh! Ugh!	Paeechah	Pah	Pah.
Hammock	Caupan	Gaban	Gaban.
To call	Eenah	Enwi	Enwah.

Many other words might be given, but the above is sufficient to show the remarkable similarity of form, and that where they do not agree as to certain letters the resemblance is preserved in the pronunciation. Every language has its own individuality in respect to that. The Welsh is noted for its deep gutturals, and, to the ear unaccustomed to hear it, it seems very harsh Travellers have observed this guttural pronunciation very extensively among the American Indians. Lossing says that the language of the Uchees, the remnant of a once powerful nation who were seated in Georgia, Alabama, Mississippi, and farther west, was exceedingly harsh, and unlike that of any other nation. Mr. Baldwin, in his recent work on "Ancient America," in his endeavors to determine the origin of the Natches Indians, says, "they differed in language, customs, and condition from all other Indians in the country." He then attempts to affix their traditions with the people of Mexico. It may be remembered that elsewhere it is stated that it was right in the midst of the territory occupied by the Natches that Mr. Willin, a rich Quaker, had among his settlers a number of Welshmen, who conversed in their native tongue with the Indians. Also, that Mr. Burnell and his son, Cradog, were part of a company who purchased forty millions of acres from the Natches and Yazous, and that both father and son, particularly the latter, understanding the Welsh language, could converse with the Indians. Is it not altogether likely, then, that the Uchees and Natches, being known to be so very different from the surrounding nations in language, spoke the same as the Mandans, and that the language of the three did not differ much from the Welsh?

Dr. Morse, in the report of his tour (printed in New Haven in 1822) among the Western Indians, performed in the behalf of the Government, in 1820, mentions, upon the information furnished by Father Reichard, of Detroit, a report that prevailed at Fort Chartres, among the old people, in 1781, that Mandan Indians had visited that post and could converse intelligibly with some Welsh soldiers then in the British army. Dr. Morse suggested the information as a hint to any person who might have an opportunity of ascertaining whether there was any affinity between the two languages. By a guidance more than human, Mr. Catlin was led into the midst of that people, and he has shown that such an affinity does exist, and has performed a service of permanent value by his contributions to the literature of a question which was thought to be a bold imposture foisted upon a credulous age by an equally credulous but more ignorant rabble. But time is making things more equal, and the sturdy defenders of Madoc's voyages and American colony are having his claims ratified in a most astonishing manner. It is very fortunate that more recent researches have brought to light the language of a people so rapidly melting away, and thus supplied an answer to the question as to how the many Welshmen who came in contact with them could understand and converse with these Welsh Bearded Indians.

12

CHAPTER XII

WELSH BLOOD IN THE AZTECS.

MEXICO and Peru were the most civilized parts of the continent when the Spaniards arrived. If it had not been for the bigoted zeal of the Spanish priests, and most signally that of Zumarraga, the abundant and astonishing national picture-writings which were the historical records of the Aztecs might still be in existence, and serve to reveal the successive links in the mighty chain of migrations of the early peoples, so that much of the mystery that still lingers in regard to their settlement and civilization could be removed But these priests looked upon those writings as the memorials of pagan idolatry, and, having collected them together, committed them to the flames, thus extinguishing in a day, as it were, the history of a once powerful empire. The historian is consequently forced to rely upon whatever fugitive pieces escaped the hands of those infamous ravagers, the study of the monumental remains, and the broken and scattered remnants of this people, scarcely recognizable, found on the Mexican plateau and in the various parts of the American territories.

According to the most authentic records which remain, the Aztecs came from the regions of the North, "the populous hive of nations in the New World, as it has been in the Old"

Clavigero, the patient and voluminous historian of New Spain, assigns the following dates to some of the most important events in the early history of Mexico:

	A.D.
The Toltecs arrived in Anahuac	648
They abandoned their country	1051
The Chichemecs arrived	1170
The Acolhuans arrived about	1200
The Aztecs or Mexicans reached Tula .	1196
They founded the Mexican Empire . .	1325
Conquest by Cortez	1521

Zurita, a celebrated jurist, whose personal experience and observation among the Aztecs extended over a period of nineteen years, and who returned to Spain in 1560, was indignant at the epithet *barbarian* as applied to the Aztecs,—an epithet, he says, "which could come from no one who had personal knowledge of the capacity of the people or their institutions, and which in some respects is quite as well merited by the European nations."

Their high degree of civilization, their remarkable advance in the knowledge and practice of the arts and sciences, so wondrously displayed in their architecture, their causeways, their temples, their homes and their adornments, their agriculture and systems of irrigation, their floating gardens and beautiful feather-work, their strange religion and military displays, must have produced an impression upon the Spaniards which they never forgot. The vast wealth of the Aztecs so excited the spirit of avarice in them, however, that, for a time, each one planned how best to enrich himself.

In complexion they were much lighter than the common American Indians. Their style of dress, which was often the most elaborate, and made from the finest materials of their own weaving, more nearly approached that of Europeans,—trousers, jacket, surtout, cloak, and cap or hat ornamented with fine feather-work. The same dress is worn by their descendants in Mexico at the present time. Their treatment of their women was not Asiatic, but resembled more that which is accorded to them by the civilized nations of the world. Their duties were domestic, and they were not degraded by servile bondage. Throughout the different cities were barber-shops, where the men assembled to have their beards shaved. No such thing was known among the American Indians.

"Quetzalcoatl, god of the air," says Prescott, "instructed them in the use of the metals, in agriculture, and the arts of government. It was the golden age. For some cause he was compelled to abandon the country. On his way he stopped at the city of Cholula, where a temple was dedicated to his worship, the massy ruins of which still form one of the most interesting relics of antiquity in Mexico. When he reached the shores of the Mexican Gulf, *he took leave of his followers, promising that he and his descendants would revisit them hereafter*, and then, entering his wizard skiff made of serpents' skins, embarked on the great ocean for the fabled land of Tlapallan [are there not here the Welsh words *lla*, place, softened into *tla*, and *pell*, distant, meaning "distant place"?] He was said to have been tall in stature, *with a white skin, long dark hair, and a flowing beard.* The Mexicans looked confidently to the return of this benevolent deity; and this remarkable tradition, deeply cherished in their hearts, prepared the way for the success of the Spaniards."

Their religion was a compound of Christianity and mythology, of spiritual refinement and ferocity. Indeed, so much was this the case that the most intelligent and judicious historians of the Aztecs could not resist the conviction that one part of their religion emanated from a comparatively refined people, while the other sprang from barbarians. Everything pointed to the doctrine that their religion had *two distinct sources.*

Some historians have erred in supposing that they indiscriminately sacrificed human beings. Their sacrifices were criminals collected from all parts of the country, kept in cages, and slain upon the same day to make a religious exhibition. This ought to be stated, so that, if possible, there might be some mitigation of their dark and bloody practices.

They recognized the existence of one God, Supreme Creator and Lord of the Universe. In their prayers they addressed Him as their God, "by whom they lived, omnipresent, who knoweth all thoughts and giveth all gifts, without whom man is as nothing, the incorporeal, invisible, one God, of perfect perfection and purity, under whose wings we find repose and a sure defence."

They made confession but once, and that usually was deferred to a late period of life. The following was the language of the confessor for the penitent: "O merciful Lord, thou knowest the secrets of all hearts, let thy forgiveness and favor descend like the pure waters of heaven, to wash away the stains from the soul. Thou knowest that this poor man has sinned, not from his own free will, but from the influence of the sign under which he was born." He then teaches charity: "Clothe the naked and feed the hungry, whatever privations it may cost thee; for, remember, their flesh is like thine, and they are men like thee."

The ceremony of naming children shows a wonderful coincidence with what are called Christian rites. The lips and bosom of the infant were sprinkled with water, and "the Lord was implored to permit the holy drops to wash away the sin that was given to it before the foundation of the world, so that the child might be born anew."

Their prayers, too, inculcated Christian morality: "Wilt thou blot us out, O Lord, forever? Is this punishment intended not for our reformation, but for our destruction? Impart to us out of thy great mercy thy gifts, which we are not worthy to receive through our own merits."

"Keep peace with all." "Bear injuries with humility. God who sees will avenge you." "He who looks curiously on a woman commits adultery with his eyes." What parallels with Scripture teachings!

The Aztec nobles had bards in their houses, who composed ballads suited to the times, and sang and played on instruments in honor of the achievements of their lord. In this is discovered a resemblance to the customs of Welsh minstrelsy.

They had also musical councils, held on special days in the presence of large public assemblies, for the trials of historians, poets, and musicians, in their respective compositions, before the monarchs of Mexico, Tezcuco, and Tlacopan. These were exactly identical with the Welsh Eisteddfods,—bardic and musical contests, which have long been and are still held in Wales, and in other countries where the descendants of the people of that country reside They had also a complete system of orders and badges resembling those in Europe. By a study of their stone calendars, they are known to have had regular divisions of time; and their years consisted of three hundred and sixty-five days. Historians relate that in the first interview of Cortez with Montezuma in his palace, the latter said that his ancestors were not the original proprietors of the land They had occupied it but a few ages, and had been led there by a great Being, *who, after giving them laws and ruling over the nation for a time, had withdrawn to the region where the sun rises.* He had declared upon his departure that he or his descendants would again visit them and resume his empire. The wonderful deeds of the Spaniards, their fair complexion, and the quarter whence they came, led him to believe that they were his descendants.

It was this tradition, inflexibly maintained by all the natives, which enabled Cortez and his followers to secure such a complete conquest throughout the Aztec empire; and yet so cruel a monster was he that he put to death the two emperors, Montezuma and Guatemozin, and nearly four millions of their subjects, in the most cruel manner. At least, this is stated by historians; possibly the number is exaggerated. At any rate, he slew an immense number.

A gentleman who was in Mexico saw in 1748, in a Spanish manuscript there, the speech which Montezuma delivered to his subjects just prior to his death, and which is probably still in existence:

"Kinsmen, Friends, Countrymen, and Subjects:

You know I have been eighteen years your sovereign and your natural king, as my illustrious predecessors and fathers were before me, and all the descendants of my race since we came from *a far distant northern nation, whose tongue and manners we yet have partly preserved.* I have been to you a father, a guardian, and a loving prince, while you have been to me faithful subjects and obedient servants.

"Let it be held in your remembrance that you have a claim to a noble descent, because you are sprung from a race of freemen and heroes, who scorned to deprive the native Mexicans of their ancient liberties, but added to their national freedom principles which do honor to human nature. Our divines have instructed you of our natural descent from a people the most renowned upon earth for liberty and valor; because of all nations they were, as our first parents told us, the only unsubdued people upon the earth by that warlike nation [Romans] whose tyranny and ambition assumed the conquest of the world; but nevertheless our great forefathers checked their ambition, and fixed limits to their conquests, although but the inhabitants of a *small island*, and but few in number, compared to the ravagers of the earth, who attempted in vain to conquer our great, glorious, and free forefathers," etc.

In the above, Montezuma and his people looked upon themselves as the descendants of freemen and heroes who had not been subdued, who were the inhabitants of a small island in the north. The description very strikingly answers to the character, manners, and principles of the Welsh, and the place as the British Island When Cortez came to their country, Montezuma was the eleventh emperor of Mexico in the Aztec line. Now, allowing an average reign to each emperor of twenty years, it will be found that Prince Madoc's arrival in this country will about coincide with the time of the establishment of this empire. This is also true with regard to the Peruvian empire. Atahualpa, who was treacherously and inhumanly put to death by the cruel and avaricious Pizarro, was the twelfth emperor of Peru in succession from Manco Capac. By the same method of calculation it will be seen that the dynasty of the Incas was established about the time of Madoc's arrival. In consequence of this, with many other proofs which cannot be introduced here, it has been maintained that he also was the founder of the Peruvian empire and civilization. John Williams, an author of no small repute, in his "Natural History of the Mineral Kingdom," vol. ii. p. 410, maintains that not only Mexico but Peru also was discovered by Madoc; that the few fair and white persons found there by the Spaniards were the descendants of Madoc's colony; and that Manco Capac and Mamma Ocello were Madoc and his wife. They are supposed to be the progenitors of the Peruvian Incas. As they were so different from the original natives in their complexions, they were thought to be the children of the sun; a sentiment which Manco might encourage for his own preservation. Mamma Ocello he thinks a corruption of Mamma Ichel, or Uchel, the Welsh for "high or stately mother." He gives it as his opinion that Madoc in his first voyage landed in the Gulf of Mexico, and that when he went back to his native country he promised those whom he left behind to return to them; but that in his second voyage he was driven by a storm from the north down as low as Brazil, and was shipwrecked near the mouth of the Amazon River; that he and his wife and the survivors sailed up that river; that after some time he arrived at Cuzco, the capital of the Peruvian empire; and that he never came to his first colony. He then assigns many reasons for his belief. It cannot be denied that some of those reasons are ingenious. The fact of Madoc or some of his followers having reached Peru is not denied; but they reached that country from the *western*, not the *eastern*, side of the continent. They went down the sea-coast west of Mexico to make explorations, or were carried against their choice by a storm to Peru, where they settled. Such a theory is in harmony with the foregoing pages, while it does not in any way conflict with the founding of that empire by Madoc.

Three South American nations ascribe their civilization and religion to three white men who appeared among them

Abbé Molina, in his "History of Chili," vol ii. book i. chap. i., says that "there is a tribe of Indians in Baroa, Chili, whose complexions are a clear white and red."

Baron Humboldt, in his "Political Essays," remarks that "in the forests of Guiana, especially near the sources of the river Oronoco, are several tribes of a whitish complexion"

Captain John Drummond, who resided in Mexico for many years in a military capacity, as an engineer, geographer, and naturalist, favored Dr. Williams, the author of the "Enquiry," with his opinion on the subject. He said that he "was fully persuaded and convinced that Madoc was one of the confederate chiefs who went upon an expedition westward from Britain about the year 1170; and that he has heard of colonies of Welsh people now existing, who, he thinks, are descendants of Madoc's people; that the emigrants were a mixture of Welsh, North Britons, and Irish, and that Madoc was naval commander."

This was not at all unlikely, since upon Madoc's return from his first voyage he made his discoveries as public as possible. The North Britons and Irish were on friendly terms with the Welsh, and all were hostile to the English Jeuan Brecva, a Bard who flourished about the year

1480, says that Rhiryd, an illegitimate son of Owen Gwynedd, and who, according to Powell, was Lord of Clochran, in Ireland, "accompanied Madoc across the Atlantic (Morwerydd) to some lands they had found there, and there dwelt." There can be no doubt, therefore, that some Irish went with Madoc to America

It is probable, too, that some Scots were in the expedition; for Captain Drummond said that at one time he was accompanied by his servant, who was a Highlander, on a journey through the country, when they came to a Mexican hut where they heard a woman singing to her child. His servant began to show signs of astonishment, and turned to the captain and told him that the woman was using words from the Erse,—the language of the Highlands in Scotland.

The captain further observed, that Don Juan de Grijalva, a Spaniard, said that "he found the Celts of Mexico, some having little or no arms, but clothed in hides; and that the fierceness of their manners and their undaunted courage resembled the old Britons, as described by Henry II. to the Emperor Emmanuel Commenes. He also found others with short-skirted vests of different colors, with targets and short black spears, and that these new men in Mexico were adored by the natives for their courage and dexterity, for that they never had seen ships till they came among them from afar."

Antonio Goluasco, a Portuguese author of great celebrity, mentions the expedition of a Captain Machan, a British adventurer, in 1344, who had been in Mexico, and had got store of wealth and silver from the native sovereign of that day, but who was cast away on his return to Europe, with all his treasure, near Madeira.

Also, from the negotiations of Sir John Hawkins, an English admiral, in the latter part of Queen Elizabeth's reign, and from the speeches of various Mexican chiefs to Sir John's officers who were sent from Vera Cruz to Mexico to negotiate with the Spanish Viceroy, is deduced strong proof that these chiefs looked upon themselves as descended from the Welsh

The Tlascalans belonged to the same great family with the Aztecs. They came on the grand Mexican plateau about the same time with the kindred races, at the close of the *twelfth* century. Their immense fortifications and walls, which extended for many miles, show the same methods of construction, in semicircular lines and overlapping one another, as those in the valleys of the Ohio and Mississippi.

Most of the historians say that the two great pyramids—teocalli—just northeast of the city of Mexico were constructed by an ancient people that came to Mexico from some country east situated on the Atlantic Ocean.

What, then, is the conclusion? That the Aztecs

were the Alligewi, who were found in Virginia and the Carolinas by Madoc's colony, and with whom the latter became amalgamated and moved westward. Being more and more pressed by the powerful Indian nations which subsequently gained control of the middle and eastern countries, they were at length obliged to abandon the Ohio and Mississippi valleys. Some portions of these people had reached, as a sort of advance-guard, the Mexican plateau before those who were left behind entirely surrendered the country The date of founding the Aztec empire—1325—necessitates this view, and Clavigero, whose table of dates has been given in another part of this chapter, places the first arrival of the Aztecs in Tula as early as 1196,—twenty-six years after the arrival of Madoc.

When this mighty migration took place, a portion, from necessity, convenience, or inclination, ascended the Missouri; and of these the Mandans are the descendants; while the main body moved in a southwest direction, leaving unmistakable traces of their progress from the Mississippi to Mexico. Some of these will be noticed in a subsequent chapter.

The Aztec empire became a controlling power on this continent, and exacted tribute for the Mexican kings from all the Indian tribes. But the Welsh element was no more in point of numbers, though they were in power, to the Aztecs than the Tartars were to the Chinese. The ships which are represented on Mexican monuments as crossing an ocean are Madoc's vessels, floating on the Atlantic from Wales to America.

Abbé Brasseur de Bourbourg, the most profound investigator in Mexican and Peruvian antiquities, says, "The native traditions generally attribute their civilization to bearded white men, who came across the ocean from the east."

CHAPTER XIII.

THE MOQUIS, MOHAVES, AND MODOCS.

SEBASTIAN CABOT, in 1495, some two or three years after the first voyage of Columbus, discovered Florida and Mexico, and found along the coast the descendants of the Welsh discoverers who eventually settled in Mexico.

Sir George Mackenzie, in a letter to his grandfather, the fourth Earl of Perth, writing on the subject of Celtic discoveries in Europe and America, cites Baronius, Scaliger, Salmasius, Lipsius, and others as authorities for believing in these early emigrations. As early as the sixteenth century are found explicit accounts of strange peoples inhabiting certain portions of America and possessing different characteristics from the aborigines. Hakluyt, in his third volume, has an extract from Antonio de Epejo, written in 1583: "The Spaniards along the Rio del Norte, latitude 37° upwards, found the Indians far more civilized, and having a better form of government, than any others in Mexico They had a great number of large and very populous towns, well built of stone and lime, three or four stories high; their country is very large and extensive. The chief town, called Cia, has not less than eight markets. The inhabitants are very warlike, have great plenty of cows and sheep, dress neat's leather very fine, and make of it shoes and boots, which no other Americans do. They have also deer-skins and chamois equal to those of Flanders (probably brought to Flanders from Switzerland), and abound with excellent provision in the greatest profusion. They have large fields of corn, and make curious things of feathers of various colors. They manufacture cotton, of which they make fine mantles, striped with blue and white. They have many salt lakes in their country, that abound with excellent fish, and from the waters of which they make excellent white salt. The country abounds with wild beasts, wild fowl, and all sorts of game. They breed great numbers of hens. The climate is very fine, the soil rich, producing great quantities of delicious fruits. They have amongst them grapes the same as those of Castile, and fine roses like those of Europe. They have also abundance of excellent metals, gold and silver. The people are very industrious and laborious, and the cultivation of the ground occupies all their time. Their houses are flat-roofed. The country is very mountainous, and has excellent timber; and the inhabitants seem to have some knowledge of the Christian faith. They have many chapels, and erect crosses, and they live in general in great security and peace. The largest lake is in the western part of the country, and around it is a great number of large, well-built, and populous towns. The people are neatly dressed, in clothes made of exceeding well-dressed skins and cotton cloth."

Captain Carver, in his "Travels in North America," says that "northwest of the Missouri and St. Pierre, the Indians farther told me that there was a nation rather smaller and whiter than the neighboring tribes, who cultivate the ground, and (as far as I could gather from their expressions) in some measure the arts. They are supposed to be some of the different tribes that were tributary to the Mexican kings, and who fled from their native country to seek an asylum in these parts about the time of the conquest of Mexico by the Spaniards, about two centuries ago."

Farther on (page 386), he says, "The Jesuits and French missionaries also pretended that the Indians had, when they first travelled into America, some notions—though these were dark and confused—of the Christian institutions, for they were greatly agitated at the sight of the cross, which made such impressions on them that showed that they were not unacquainted with the sacred mysteries of Christianity."

Very little has been known until late years of the Rio del Norte and its source or sources, which flows in a southerly direction through New

Mexico and empties into the Gulf But as the population has increased in this country with astonishing rapidity, and settlements have been opened in the Territories, and there was a necessity for a well-organized Indian Bureau to provide for the scattered tribes living in the Southwest, the condition and character of the country and of the people in New Mexico, Colorado, and Arizona are being brought to light. Military and scientific expeditions have been sent into those countries, which have returned with reports of having discovered new nations about whom nothing has been hitherto known.

In the campaign of General Crook against the Apaches, a large tract of country, rich with the relics of the past, was opened. It contains a chain of cities in ruins and ancient towns still inhabited by a race which holds itself aloof from Mexicans, Indians, and Americans, and prides itself on its descent from the ancient inhabitants of the country, and maintains a religion and government peculiar to itself The largest settlement was found in Mexico, about thirty miles south of the border line. A strong wall surrounds it Within are houses for about four thousand people. The population had dwindled at the time they were discovered to about eighteen hundred Montezuma is their deity, and his coming is looked for at sunrise each day Their priests wear heavily-embroidered robes, while their religious ceremonies are very formal and pompous. They have a high order of morality. The chief powers of government are vested in thirteen caciques, six of whom are elected for life. They are quite advanced in civilization. Their women are not treated as beasts of burden, but are respected, and permitted to confine themselves to housekeeping. From all that can be gleaned, it appears that these people have maintained their traditions unbroken for at least three centuries and a half.

Alvar Nuñez Cabeza de Baca published, in 1529, a description of his wanderings in America. He was in New Mexico, and, in writing of the Indian villages, said, "The New Mexico pueblos—villages—are generally two stories high, with doors on the roof and the staircase ladders on the outside." Within a circle of sixty miles from Santa Fé there are to be found the ruins of over forty deserted towns; and in various other portions of New Mexico and Arizona similar ruins are in existence, all showing that there once resided here a powerful people essentially differing from the common American Indians. They were not placed here by the Spaniards, but had occupied these towns and cities long before their coming. By some it is believed that Montezuma originated in New Mexico; and some even designate his birthplace. Some locate it at the old pueblo of Pecos; while others maintain that it was near Ojo Caliente, the ruins of which are still to be seen. A document is now extant purporting to be copied from one of the legends at the capital in Mexico, in which it is stated that Montezuma was born in Teguayo, one of the ancient pueblos of New Mexico. This was not his original name, but was applied to him upon his elevation to the Aztec throne, as it was to his predecessors. It is supposed by some that in this region was situated the Aztlan, whence came the Aztecs to Mexico; by others that it was along the Gila River, in Arizona. But throughout that entire country the ancient towns which are now inhabited and the deserted ruins show a common origin.

The view has been entertained by some who have given this subject attention that it was at this point in the progress of the migrations that Madoc and his followers finally became amalgamated with the Aztecs.

Within the past few years, several visits have been made by the members of Wheeler's Surveying Expedition—Samuel Woodworth Cozzens and a few others—to the seven wonderful cities of the Moquis, situated near the Colorado Chiquito, in Arizona.

Dr Oscar Leow, chemist to Wheeler's Surveying Expedition, has contributed a brief but intensely interesting article to the "Popular Science Monthly" for July, 1874, on "The Moquis Indians of Arizona." By reference to the Indian reports, it appears that this nation has never been brought in contact with the Indian Bureau, nor with the Arizona agency, although within its jurisdiction. Small appropriations have recently been made for them; and it is likely that much more will soon be learned about them,—their habits, industries, language, and strange history.

Their seven cities stand upon very high, precipitous cliffs of sandstone, which, when seen in the distance, present such bold fronts that it appears out of the question for any one to think of climbing them. As the traveller approaches, however, he discovers narrow and circuitous paths, which must be passed over single file, up and up, till the summit is reached. On this giddy height is the home of the Moquis. Dr. Leow terms it the "Gibraltar of the West," which the Navajos and Apaches have never been able to conquer. The Moquis number about two thousand five hundred. The cities rest on four sandstone *mesas*,—tables,—which are about eight miles apart On the first table are three of the cities, named Tehua, Tsitsumo-vi, and Obiki; on the second are Mushangene-vi and Shebaula-vi; the third is Shongoba-vi; and on the fourth is Orai-vi.

The houses are built in rows of two, three, and four stories in height, and constructed in terrace style, with the upper stories removed a few feet back from the lower ones. The sides fronting the bluffs are quite near, with only a narrow ledge along which to walk, and where the children were seen by the doctor, playing, unconscious of danger, while the mothers were within the houses performing their duties, though an awful gulf hundreds of feet in depth yawned beneath Here the habitations are not built of adobe, like Indian and Mexican huts, but of stones firmly held in place by a cement of clay and sand. The stories are about seven feet high, divided into rooms, and each provided with a fire-place. Windows are cut into the walls about a foot square.

The architecture of these stone houses bears a marked conformity with that of the ruder ages among the Welsh.

The physical appearance of the Moquis is a nearer approach to that of the Caucasian than to that of the Mongolian race. The complexion is a light red-brown, and the countenance unusually intelligent.

Mr. Cozzens says that "their faces were so bright and intelligent that I fancied they only required to be clothed in American dress, and shorn of their long locks of coarse black hair, to enable them to easily pass for people of our own race who had become brown from exposure to the sun.

"Their clothing is neat, and they have an abundance of it. They knit, spin, and weave blankets, cloaks, etc. They also manufacture certain kinds of pottery. They have a system of reservoirs or stone tanks, built of masonry in a substantial manner, and which hold millions of gallons of water.

These are connected with smaller ones below by pipes, and thus utilized for their stock, which comprise dogs, donkeys, sheep, goats, and chickens. The sheep and goats are driven some eight or ten miles from the mesas to some pasture-lands. The principal crop is corn, which is planted deep in the ground to obtain a greater degree of moisture. The corn is ground, and then mixed with water, so as to form a pastē. The woman who makes it dips her hand in the paste and rapidly passes some of it over hot stones, where it is soon baked. The cakes resemble the Welsh *bara llechan*, noted in their cookery. They have a kind of food called *panoche*, and still another called *tom iles*,—by mixing flour and meat in a powdered state. They also raise beans, cotton, and tobacco.

"The women appear more intelligent than the men, and dress with far more taste. The daughters of the chief are said to be exceedingly interesting ladies. The hair is worn à la Pompadour, with two inverse rolls on the side of the head, by the unmarried. When married, the rolls give place to broad braids. The Moquis girls have one privilege which ladies do not generally enjoy: they have the right to propose for their own husbands. When they have made their proposals, the fathers make the arrangements. The bride then prepares with her own hands the wedding-dinner.

"Females are not permitted to dance; their places are taken by young men who dress in imitation of the women. All the dancers wear masks made of peeled willow twigs nicely woven together; males have theirs dyed brown, and supposed females bright yellow.

"The vice of drunkenness and crime of murder are not known among this people.

"They are kind, warm-hearted, and hospitable. They believe that their great father, Montezuma, lives where the sun rises."

Mr. Cozzens studied their manners and customs, and endeavored to learn something of the history of this singular race He says that it is asserted by the people of the other pueblos "that they are descendants of the Aztecs, though with Welsh blood in their veins."

That they have occupied their present location for a long time may be inferred from the fact that their feet have worn down the path in the rock between the several villages to the depth of some inches.

The Mohaves, who are on the Colorado River Reservation, Arizona, are a small, isolated tribe, not more than perhaps a thousand all told. They are different from all other Indians. The women are tall, cleanly, and less servile than most Indian women. Their language is peculiar, and has Welsh words in it. The more recent reports of the United States Government agents contain complaints against the vile traders who are leading this once sober and respectable tribe into all sorts of vice, drunkenness, immorality, loathsome diseases, and crimes. White men, with their boasted civilization and virtues, drag the Indians to the brink of ruin, and then crowd them over as vile and disgusting creatures.

The perfidious and barbarous massacre of General Canby, Rev. Eleazer Thomas, and others, by that savage band called the Modocs, brought them into an unenviable notoriety, but, while passing, it is worthy of query how they came by a name so much like that of Madoc.

CHAPTER XIV.

SIGNS OF FREEMASONRY AMONG INDIANS.

THE first printed evidence of the introduction of Freemasonry in America is found in the "Pennsylvania Gazette" of December 8th, 1730, published by Benjamin Franklin. It is as follows: "As there are several lodges of Freemasons erected in this province, and people have been lately much amused with conjectures concerning them, we think the following account of Freemasonry from London will not be unacceptable to our readers." This is followed by a letter on the mystery. But, if the testimony of intelligent travellers can be accepted, it seems quite evident that lodges of Freemasons were in existence among the American Indians centuries prior to this time, all of which point to a Welsh origin. They certainly had private societies, which met at certain times, and the proceedings of which were kept inviolably secret under an oath.

Governor De Witt Clinton believed that the signs of Freemasonry were found among the Indians. He was an eminent member of the craft himself, and was as familiar with its history, government, rules, and signs as any person of his time. In an interview that he had with an Indian preacher, the latter unmistakably made revelations which convinced the former that he was familiar with the order. This Indian said that he had obtained this knowledge from a Menomonie chief.

There was one order among the Iroquois consisting of five Oneidas, two Cayugas, two St Regis, and six Senecas. The period of their meeting could never be ascertained. These private societies were not confined to the Iroquois, but seem to have extended among all the tribes. Their rules of government and the admission of members were the same as among the whites. No one could be received as a member of the fraternity except by ballot, and the concurrence of the whole body was necessary to a choice. They had different degrees in the order. Their ceremonies of initiation were remarkable, and the mode of passing from one degree to another would awaken astonishment among civilized Masons.

Whence did they originate? There was a long period in Europe when the knowledge of Freemasonry was mostly confined to the Druids, and in Wales this order was the most generally found. It was their home. There they had their colleges and schools of learning. They were, indeed, priests, legislators, and historians. Through their order the principles of the mystic craft were preserved throughout Europe. It was associated with the later system of Bardism; and when under James the First there was such a revival of the order, and it began to spread with such rapidity, embracing all classes, from the king on his throne down to his humblest subject, it was known that its deepest roots were struck in the soil of Wales. Madoc, the son of a king, and surrounded by a heroic band of eminent men, could not be ignorant of the principles of Freemasonry, and when they landed in America they brought those principles with them, to be afterwards imparted to such of those with whom they mingled as to offer material means of safety. There are not wanting instances where the lives of many whites have been spared by the Indians because they understood certain secret signs communicated to them.

CHAPTER XV.

THE WELSH LANGUAGE AMONG AMERICAN INDIANS.

AN eminent modern linguist has said "that the genealogy and antiquities of nations can be learned only from the sure testimony of their languages." Admitting the correctness of such a statement, though it does not possess axiomatic accuracy, it may furthermore be added, that the discovery of portions of a language among other distant nations, separated by a vast ocean, and differing in race, language, habits, and conditions of life, surely indicates that some who spoke that language must have brought it there. It may be urged that distant resemblances have led enthusiastic philologists in support of their cause to imagine a similarity in the form and sound of certain words, when, in fact, those words are entirely different in meaning. Instances of this kind have occurred in the study of the European languages. But when it is found that an identity exists in (1) the form, (2) the sound, and (3) the signification, and that, too, in multiplied instances, there is reason to believe that this identity does not rest on accident or coincidence. The student of language searches for some more satisfactory solution of the question, by ascertaining, if possible, how those portions were introduced

Now, this is just the case with the Celtic language found among the Indian dialects From New England to South America, Celtic words have been found whose structure, pronunciation, and signification were the same as those in use by the Gaels, Erse or Irish, and Welsh. Names of tribes, persons, places, rivers, and of many living and inanimate objects on the American continent, have been applied, and are now used, which can find their right place only by assigning to them a Celtic origin. This very soon came to be observed by all Europeans who arrived in the country, and some set themselves diligently to work to find out the cause. Some said that was not to be wondered at,—the finding of Celtic words among Americans,—for undoubtedly the Celts have been very widely spread over the globe. This, however, was too general an affirmation to satisfy others. The celebrated Bishop Nicholson believed that the Welsh language formed a considerable part of the languages of the American nations Sir Thomas Herbert, who published his travels in London in 1683, has given a list of words taken from the Indian dialects, which have an undoubted Welsh origin: *groeso*, "welcome," *gwenddwr*, "white or limpid water," *bara*, "bread," *tad*, "father," *mam*, "mother," *buch* or *buwch*, "cow," *llwynog*, "fox," *coch y dwr*, "a red water-bird," *clugjar* (American, *clugar*), "partridge." Some doubt the derivation of "penguin" from *pengwyn*, because it is thought that "white head"—its literal meaning—would be a misnomer when applied to the American penguin. By no means. As it stands on its short legs it presents a white front from its head and exposed breast, and might very well have received this appellation. There is some similarity in the name of a once powerful chief who lived in New England to that of Madoc, viz., Madokawando,—Madoc and *gwrando*, "to listen" or "to be obedient to," "to submit to or follow." The guttural *g* in the Welsh language is often dropped, especially before a vowel. Take the Welsh verb *gallu*, "to be able," or the noun *gall*, "energy, might," and by the omission of the letter *g* the words will stand *allu*, *all*. *U* is sounded like *e* in English, hence *allu* would be pronounced alle. Alligeni (Alleghany) is a compound word, composed of *allu*, "mighty," and *geni*, "born," or "mighty born" This is the name of the people who once dwelt along the immense range called by that name, and were displaced by the powerful nations, particularly the Iroquois, who came from the northwest. Potomac has a more evident Greek origin, for its word for "river" is *potamos*. Pontigo seems to come from *pont*, "a bridge," and *go*, "a smith,"—"a smith's bridge." Nanticoke is found in *nant-y-cwch*, "a curved brook or river,"—a very appropriate designation for that tribe, whether applied prior to their leaving the river in Maryland or after ascending the Susquehanna.

Appomattox—now well known to the world—signifies *appwy*, "appoint" or "name," and *Mattox*, "Madoc" or "Mattoc," the latter having the soft Silurian sound; hence, "Madoc's name."

Madoc's Creek is known by most Virginians, and by others.

It is well known that in the origin of Indian names it was customary for the tribes to assume those of the country they inhabited which had some distinct peculiarities. By this means, as they removed from one place to another, these names became multiplied. For example, the U-in-tats, known as a branch of the Utes, belonged to the Uintah Valley. U-imp is the name for pine; U-im-too-meap, pine-land, which, contracted, means U-in-tahs. The origin of Ute is as follows: U is a term signifying arrow; U-too-meap, arrow-land, because the country bordering Utah Lake furnished the reeds for arrow-shafts.

Aztlan seems clearly to have been derived from Welsh words having become mingled with Indian dialects, as *as*, "plane surface" or "area," and *lan*, "up," an elevated area or table-land. What better definition could be found to describe the Aztec plateau, beginning in Aztlan proper and continuing to widen into the Mexican plateau? The termination *lan* is very common in the Aztec language. It is found in the names of tribes, their cities, and a multitude of other objects,—Tlascalans, Cholulans, and other peoples who dwelt in and around the upper countries of the Aztec empire. The terminations *an* and *pan*, the latter indicating locality, as prefix or suffix, are very noticeable. So frequent also is the use of *ch*, *th*, and *ll*, that the Welsh student who speaks or reads aloud Aztec words is simply astounded by their perfect consonance with those of his native tongue.

Rev. Morgan Jones affirms that in 1660 he conversed with Indians who spoke and understood the Welsh language, that he remained among them and preached in that language four months, and that it was his intention when he left to return and visit them. Rev. Charles Beatty, General Bowles, Messrs. Price, Binon, Willin, Burnell, Griffith, Stuart, Sevier, Lewis, and many others unhesitatingly relate that they personally, or those whom they knew to be veracious, intelligent witnesses, had visited Indians who spoke the Welsh language sufficiently to be understood by them, without taking into account their other peculiarities of color, beard, customs, traditions, arts, etc.

George Catlin, who spent years of patient investigation into the language of the Mandans and of other Indians, has given a table of Mandan and Welsh words, with their pronunciations. Those who have any acquaintance with the Moquis and Mohave tongues declare that they contain Welsh words. Relics with Celtic inscriptions have been unearthed. Aztec and Spanish chroniclers confirm more recent researches respecting the presence of Celtic words in the old Aztec language. The speech of Montezuma discloses their eastern origin, and that their astounding civilization was due to white men.

What then?

Why, that such a mass of testimony under such a variety of circumstances, precluding the idea of preconcert, interest, prejudice, or downright ignorance, establishes the fact that the Welsh were on this continent prior to its discovery by Columbus, and that those Welsh were led thither by Prince Madoc in 1170 A D. Many historical facts to which the world has given implicit credence are far less supported than the above. Hereafter let not American historians pass over these facts in contemptuous silence.

CHAPTER XVI.

THE WELSH OF THE AMERICAN REVOLUTION.

THE Welsh have claims for recognition and patriotic gratitude by the American people, because of the prominent part taken by some of their descendants in founding the American Republic. The Welsh mind and heart have contributed no small share, in common with the good, the noble, and the enlightened of other lands, to mould its institutions and to make possible a country where the highest conditions of a Christian civilization may be enjoyed.

That little vessel of one hundred and eighty tons' burden, the Mayflower, embryo of a free republic, was commanded by a Welshman, Captain Jones. Among those who came as passengers were several of Welsh origin,—Thomas Rogers, Stephen Hopkins, John Alden, and John Howland. The last one named was attached to Governor Carver's household. So the Welsh have a share in the celebration of the landing of the Pilgrim Fathers. What must have been the thoughts of that band of forty-one men (one hundred and one souls in all) as they stood on Plymouth Rock and looked into the vast forests before them, so soon by their sturdy energy and that of their descendants to be transformed into fruitful farms and splendid cities and towns!

Roger Williams was born in Wales in 1599. He was a relative of the Protector, Oliver Cromwell. Banished from Massachusetts in 1635, he penetrated the forests in mid-winter till he came to the country of the Narragansets,—where the chief sachem, Canonicus, gave him a grant of land, which, in token of "God's merciful providence to him in his distress," he called Providence. Here he established a pure democracy, all equally sharing the dignity and privileges of the government. He was so kind in his treatment of the surrounding Indians that he was much beloved by them, and it was by his great power over them that he saved his white persecutors from destruction. Yet his enemies did not revoke his sentence of banishment. The city government of Providence is honoring his memory by the erection of a bronze statue.

Of that immortal band of men who composed the Continental Congress, and were signers of the Declaration of Independence, eighteen were Welshmen:

John Adams . . . . Massachusetts.
Samuel Adams . . . "

Stephen Hopkins . .	Rhode Island.
William Williams . .	Connecticut.
William Floyd . . .	New York.
Francis Lewis . . .	" "
Lewis Morris . . .	" "
Francis Hopkinson . .	New Jersey.
Robert Morris . . .	Pennsylvania.
George Clymer . . .	"
John Morton . . .	"
John Penn	North Carolina.
Arthur Middleton . .	South Carolina.
Button Gwinnett . .	Georgia.
Thomas Jefferson . .	Virginia.
Benjamin Harrison . .	"
Richard Henry Lee . .	"
Francis Henry Lightfoot Lee	"

Notwithstanding abler pens have sketched them all, it may not be uninteresting to touch upon a few facts in the biography of the above list. Commencing with New England, where so many of Welsh blood came after the Restoration, having been the followers of Cromwell, it will be in order to notice John and Samuel Adams.

John Adams was born at Quincy, Massachusetts, in 1735. His services were distinguished in the American Revolution; he was a member of the committee which made the draft of the Declaration, and a signer of the document. He was President and Vice-President of the United States. He died at the age of ninety-one, in 1826, just half a century after the Declaration.

Samuel Adams was born in Boston, in 1722. He was a fearless patriot and a stirring orator. He was educated for the ministry at Harvard College, but became so engrossed in politics that he relinquished that profession He was in the Continental Congress, was Governor of Massachusetts, and left the impress of his power on the Constitution of his State, which he helped to frame. He died at the age of eighty-one, in 1803.

Stephen Hopkins was born in Providence, and was a self-taught man. He wrote and acted against the oppression of the colonies by the home-government long prior to the Revolution. He filled important offices in his State, became a member of the Continental Congress, and signed the Declaration. He died in July, 1785.

From Connecticut came William Williams. He graduated at Harvard College, at the age of twenty, in 1751. He became a lawyer, but afterwards chose the profession of arms, and was aide to his brother who fell at Fort George in 1755. He died at the age of eighty-one, in 1811.

New York furnished three Welshmen out of her four delegates,—the fourth, Mr. Livingston, being of Scotch origin, though the family came from Holland. William Floyd was born in the year 1734, on Long Island. He was possessed of large means. He was in the first Continental Congress in 1774, and signed the Declaration in 1776. His losses of property by the English were large. He died at the age of eighty-seven, in 1821.

Francis Lewis was born in South Wales, in 1713. His education was partly acquired in Scotland and in Westminster, London. He was in business in that city, came to New York, and conducted business for English merchants. He was taken prisoner in the French War and carried to France; after his return to New York he was sent to Congress, and signed the Declaration in 1776. His property on Long Island was destroyed by the English. He died at the age of ninety, in 1803

Lewis Morris, the fourth and last from New York, was born of a Welsh family, in 1726. He was a graduate of Yale, and afterwards settled on his father's farm, now known as Morrisania, Westchester County. Lewis's father was the son of an officer in Cromwell's army, and first royal governor of New Jersey, in 1738. Lewis was sent to the Continental Congress in 1775, and served till 1777. His losses by the Revolution were immense. He died at the age of seventy-two, in 1798.

Francis Hopkinson, a delegate from New Jersey, was from a Welsh family. He was born in Philadelphia, in 1737. He was noted as a lawyer, wit, and poet. He wrote several political pamphlets, and was the author of many poetical *jeux-d'esprit*, one of the best-known of which is "The Battle of the Kegs," which begins,—

"Gallants, attend, and hear a friend
Trill forth harmonious ditty,
Strange things I'll tell, which late befell
In Philadelphia City."

Mr. Hopkinson signed the Declaration, afterwards was eminent as a judge, and died at the age of fifty-three, in 1791. His son, Joseph Hopkinson, was the author of the national song "Hail Columbia," the origin of which was as follows. It was in 1798 The country was excited in anticipation of war with France. Mr. Fox, a theatrical singer and actor, called upon Mr. Hopkinson and remarked, "To-morrow evening is appointed for my benefit at the theatre. Not a single box has been taken, and I fear there will be a thin house. If you will write some patriotic verse to the tune of the 'President's March,' I feel sure of a full house." Mr. Hopkinson went to his study, wrote the first verse and chorus, then submitted them to Mr. Fox, who sang them to a harpsichord accompaniment. The song was completed, the next morning the placards announcing that Mr. Fox would sing a new patriotic song. The theatre was crowded, the song was sung, and the audience thrilled with patriotic delight.

The name of George Clymer indicates his Welsh origin. Thomas Jefferson boarded in the house of Mrs. Clymer, on the southwest corner of Seventh and High Streets, Philadelphia, where he drew the original draft of the Declaration.

John Morton, although a resident of Pennsylvania, was born in Delaware, and was descended from a Welsh family on his mother's side. His father was of Swedish descent. He was on the committee which reported the Articles of Confederation.

John Penn, of a Welsh family, was born in Virginia. He studied law with Mr Pendleton, and subsequently settled in North Carolina. From there he was sent as delegate, and signed the Declaration.

Arthur Middleton, from South Carolina, was a Welshman. He was a graduate of Cambridge University, England, and arrived in America in 1773. He was taken prisoner when Charleston surrendered to the British. He lost most of his fortune by the Revolution. He died in January, 1789, aged forty-four.

Button Gwinnett was a native of Wales. He was born in 1732, was well educated, entered mercantile life, went to Georgia and purchased a large tract of land. He signed the Declaration, aided in framing the State Constitution, was Governor, and fell in a duel which he fought with General McIntosh, aged forty-six.

Thomas Jefferson's ancestors came from the foot of Mount Snowdon, Wales, to the colony of Virginia. He boasted of his Welsh blood. He stands in the front as a defender of civil and religious liberty, and had engraved upon his seal, "*Resistance to tyrants is obedience to God.*"

As the author of the Declaration, of the abolition of the connection between Church and State, the laws of primogeniture, the restrictions upon the Federal Constitution respecting the States, so as forever to prevent a centralized and an aristocratic government, he must be recognized as one of the most valuable men this country has ever had. By a strange coincidence—shall it be called that? —at the age of eighty-four, he breathed his last on the same day that John Adams did, July 4, 1826. They were life-long personal friends, with a brief interruption, but political opponents. On a plain marble slab at Monticello is the following inscription:

HERE LIES THOMAS JEFFERSON:
Author of the Declaration of Independence;
of the Statute of Virginia for Religious Freedom;
and Father of the University of Virginia.

Benjamin Harrison, chairman of the Committee that reported the Declaration, was descended from the Welsh. He was related to General Thomas Harrison, one of the regicides, the Commonwealth men of Cromwell, and who was executed at Newgate. When he was approaching the scaffold, one of the king's scoffers stood by and tauntingly asked, "Where is your good old cause now?" The brave Harrison, with a cheerful smile, replied, clapping his hand on his breast, "*Here it is, and I am going to seal it with my blood."* Some of that grand stuff was afterwards found in his descendants. Benjamin Harrison filled various positions, and was Governor of the State from 1782 to 1784. He died on his farm in 1790. His son, William Henry Harrison, served in the War of 1812, and was elected President of the United States in 1840, but died on the 4th of April, 1841, precisely one month after his inauguration.

Richard Henry Lee was from a Welsh family, as, in fact, were all the Lees of that period. He was born in 1732, educated in England, and after his return to America in 1757 was elected a member of the House of Burgesses.

He was elected to the Continental Congress in 1774, and in July, 1776, he had the honor to offer the resolution declaring the colonies free and independent. The day before the appointment of the committee to draft the Declaration, Mr. Lee was called away to the bedside of a sick wife, or he would doubtless have been appointed chairman. In 1773 he, Thomas Jefferson, and Patrick Henry had a serious consultation in the old Raleigh Tavern, at Williamsburg, Virginia, in respect to submitting a resolution to the Virginia House, recommending the appointment of a Committee of Vigilance and Correspondence, and expressing the hope that the other colonies would do the same. It was passed; and from that time the Revolution began to assume organic form, and prepared the way for 1776. Mr. Lee was United States Senator under the Constitution, which office he held with signal ability. He died June 14, 1794, in his sixty-second year.

Francis Henry Lightfoot Lee was of Welsh origin, and a signer. He was born in Virginia on the 10th of September, 1734. He was educated at home, and from 1765 to 1775 served his State as a member of the House of Burgesses. He died in April, 1797, in his sixty-third year.

Many of the facts given above concerning these signers are not found in their usual biographies, and therefore they are inserted here.

Robert Morris, who came to this country when a child, served an apprenticeship with a merchant, became a successful business man by his energy and integrity, and during the Revolution his fortune and unlimited commercial credit were superior to Congress itself. In the darkest days, when the army was unfed and unclothed, Washington could turn to his dear friend Robert Morris for help. He gave his immense means to his country, and died, in comparative poverty, in 1806, aged seventy-three years.

Gouverneur Morris, who wrote the first connected draft of the American Constitution, was a Welshman.

Among those who fought in the Revolution may be found a long list of Welsh by nativity or descent:

GENERALS.

Charles Lee,	Daniel Morgan,
Isaac Shelby,	John Cadwallader,
Anthony Wayne,	Andrew Lewis,
Morgan Lewis,	Otho H. Williams,
William R. Davie,	John Thomas,
Edward Stevens,	Joseph Williams,
Richard Winn,	James Reese.

COLONELS.

David Humphreys,	Henry Lee,
Lambert Cadwallader,	Thomas Marshall,
Richard Howell,	James Williams (*killed at Bennington*).
Ethan Allen,	

CAPTAINS.

John Marshall (*afterwards Chief Justice*),	Isaac Davis,
	Anthony Morris,
Captain Rogers.	

Besides these, there was a host of subordinate officers who could claim descent from the Welsh.

In the navy were Commodore Hopkins and others; and at a later period Commodores Rogers, Perry, Jacob Jones, and Ap Catesby Jones.

Dr. John Morgan was Surgeon-in-Chief of the American army, and one of the founders of the Philadelphia Medical School, the first of the kind established in America, and the beginning of the great University. He came from a Welsh family.

Among the divines were Revs. David Jones, Samuel Davie, David Williams, Morgan Edwards, and others. Perhaps the most distinguished of these was Mr. Jones. His ancestors came from Wales, and settled on the "Welsh Tract" in Delaware county, Pa. He was on a mission among the Shawanese and Delaware Indians in 1772-73 In 1776 he was appointed chaplain to Colonel St. Clair's regiment, and was on duty at Ticonderoga when the enemy was momentarily expected from Crown Point. He delivered a characteristic discourse, which produced a powerful impression upon the troops. When with General Wayne, he saw an English dragoon alight and enter a house for refreshments. The chaplain went to the dragoon's horse, took the pistols from the holsters, went into the house, made him a prisoner, and marched him into camp: Wayne complimented him for his bravery. He was also with General Gates; also at the battles of Brandywine, Germantown, and Monmouth; with the army at Valley Forge, and in all subsequent campaigns to the surrender of Yorktown by Cornwallis. At the age of seventy-six he served as chaplain in the War of 1812. He died in February, 1820, aged eighty-four.

Rev. Samuel Davies became President of Princeton College. When Washington was colonel, and after Braddock's defeat, Mr. Davies, who was addressing the volunteer company, used this language in allusion to Washington: "I cannot but hope that Providence has hitherto preserved him in so signal a manner for some important service to his country."

General Washington's family associations were with the descendants of the Welsh. His wife, Martha, whom he called familiarly "Patsy," was the grand-daughter of Rev. Orlando Jones, who came to Virginia from Wales. Colonel Fielding Lewis, of Welsh descent, married Washington's sister; and his son, George Washington Lewis, was commander of the general's life-guard.

Elihu Yale, the founder of Yale College, Jonathan Edwards, Daniel Webster, Charles Davies the mathematician, and a long array of brilliant men and women who have adorned every station in American society, were of Welsh origin or descent. Mr. Webster, however, was descended only from his mother's side.

Seven Presidents of the United States have descended from the Welsh race,—John Adams, Thomas Jefferson, James Madison, James Monroe, John Quincy Adams, and William Henry Harrison.

Chief-Justice John Marshall, the first to expound the Constitution, was the grandson of a native of Wales; and, as if the office should continue in such a lineage, Chief-Justice Roger B. Taney was sprung from a family descended from the northern part of Wales.

William Penn, founder of the great State of

Pennsylvania, Thomas Floyd, the first Governor of the colony, and Anthony Morris, the first mayor of the refined city of Philadelphia, were Welsh.

Oliver Evans, so famous for his inventions in high-pressure engines, by means of which all turbid streams could be successfully navigated, was born of a Welsh family near that city. It was found that the sediment of the water choked up or wore off the sliding-valves of the low-pressure engines. He was the third person who received a patent from the United States—Samuel Hopkins being the first for his inventions, and concerning which President Jefferson remarked that they were "too valuable to be covered by a patent, for they were such things that the people could not do without, once they were known"

Mrs. De Witt Clinton was the daughter of Dr. Thomas Jones, the son of a Welsh physician whose father settled at Jamaica, Long Island, and who was widely known as Dr. John Jones. He was attached to the Revolutionary army as a surgeon, and a personal friend of Washington and Franklin. He was one of the founders of the New York Hospital, and a professor in the medical faculty in Columbia College at its institution. He was the first successful lithotomist in the country Mrs. Clinton was his granddaughter, having Dr. Thomas Jones for her father, and a daughter of Philip Livingston, signer of the Declaration, for her mother. Maturin Livingston, a son of Philip, married a daughter of General Morgan Lewis. Of Mrs. Clinton it has been said that "she was in every sense a remarkable woman,—not less for her strength of mind than for her noble good breeding, purity, and polish of manners She was liberal and frank, and fully appreciated the great mind of her noble husband; and the harder the storms of personal and political strife blew upon him, the closer her affections twined around him, while she nobly and devoutly cherished his memory to the last"

Their services, in connection with those of almost every other land, have helped to lay the foundations, deep and broad, of the great American republic, whose majestic proportions are rising higher and still higher, commanding the wonder and admiration of all; but, while the later builders are at work, they will not forget to offer some souvenir in behalf of those who worked so wisely and so well.

The memory of ALL "smells sweet, and blossoms in the dust."

CHAPTER XVII.

ADDRESS OF REV. DAVID JONES TO GENERAL ST. CLAIR'S BRIGADE, AT TICONDEROGA, WHEN THE ENEMY WERE HOURLY EXPECTED, OCTOBER 20, 1776.

"MY countrymen, fellow-soldiers, and friends:

"I am sorry that during this campaign I have been favored with so few opportunities of addressing you on subjects of the greatest importance, both with respect to this life and that which is to come; but what is past cannot be recalled, and now time will not admit an enlargement, as we have the greatest reason to expect the advancement of our enemies as speedily as Heaven will permit. [The wind blew strongly to the north.] Therefore, at present let it suffice to bring to your remembrance some necessary truths.

"It is our common faith, and a very just one too, that all events on earth are under the notice of that God in whom we live, move, and have our being: therefore we must believe that in this important struggle with the worst of enemies he has assigned us our post here at Ticonderoga. Our situation is such that, if properly defended, we shall give our enemies a fatal blow, and in a great measure prove the means of the salvation of North America. Such is our present case, that we are fighting for all that is near and dear to us, while our enemies are engaged in the worst of causes, their design being to subjugate, plunder, and enslave a free people that have done them no harm. Their tyrannical views are so glaring, their cause so horribly bad, that there still remains too much goodness and humanity in Great Britain to engage unanimously against us: therefore they have been obliged—and at a most amazing expense, too—to hire the assistance of a barbarous, mercenary people, that would cut your throat for the small reward of a sixpence. No doubt these have hopes of being our task-masters, and would rejoice at our calamities.

"Look, oh, look, therefore, at your respective States, and anticipate the consequences if these vassals are suffered to enter! It would fail the most fruitful imagination to represent in a proper light what anguish, what horror, what distress, would spread over the whole! See, oh, see the dear wives of your bosoms forced from their peaceful habitations, and perhaps used with such indecency that modesty would forbid the description! Behold, the fair virgins of your land, whose benevolent souls are now filled with a thousand good wishes and hopes of seeing their admirers return home crowned with victory, would not only meet with a doleful disappointment, but also with such insults and abuses that would induce their tender hearts to pray for the shades of death! See your children exposed as vagabonds to all the calamities of this life! Then, oh, then adieu to all felicity this side of the grave! Now, all these calamities must be prevented if our God be for us,—and who can doubt of this who observes the point in which the wind now blows?—if you will only acquit yourselves like men, and with firmness of mind go forth against your enemies, *resolving either to return with victory or to die gloriously*.

"Every one who may fall in this dispute will be justly esteemed a martyr to liberty, and his name will be had in precious memory while the love of freedom remains in the breasts of men. All whom God will favor to see a glorious victory will return to their respective States with every mark of honor, and be received with joy and gladness of heart by all friends to liberty and lovers of mankind. As our present case is singular, I hope, therefore, that the candid will excuse me if I conclude with an uncommon address, in substance principally extracted from the writings of the Bible, though at the same time it is freely acknowledged that I am not possessed of any similar power either of blessing or cursing.

"1. Blessed be that man who is possessed of a true love of liberty; and let all the people say, *Amen*.

"2. Blessed be that man who is a friend to the United States of America; and let all the people say, *Amen.*

"3. Blessed be that man who will use his utmost endeavors to oppose the tyranny of Great Britain, and to vanquish all her forces invading North America; and let all the people say, *Amen.*

"4. Blessed be that man who is resolved never to submit to Great Britain; and let all the people say, *Amen.*

"5. Blessed be that man who in the present dispute esteems not his life too good to fall a sacrifice in defence of his country: let his posterity, if any he has, be blessed with riches, honor, virtue, and true religion, and let all the people say, *Amen.*

"Now, on the other hand, as far as is consistent with the Holy Scriptures, let all these blessings be turned into curses to him who deserts the noble cause in which we are engaged, and turns his back to the enemy before he receives proper orders to retreat; and let all the people say, *Amen.*

"Let him be abhorred by all the United States of America.

"Let faintness of heart and fear never forsake him on earth.

"Let him be a *major miserabile*, a terror to himself and all around him.

"Let him be accursed in his outgoings, and cursed in his incomings; cursed in his lying down, and cursed in his uprising; cursed in basket, and cursed in store.

"Let him be cursed in all his connections, till his wretched head, with dishonor, is laid low in the dust; and let all the soldiers say, *Amen.*

"And may the God of all grace, in whom we live, enable us, in defence of our country, to acquit ourselves like men, to his honor and praise. *Amen* and *Amen*"

There were no traitors or cowards *that* day; and the deeds of the patriots have been emblazoned in prose and song, in monuments of brass and stone, in a great and glorious government, and in the praise and gratitude of a free people who meet to do them honor.

THE END.

CPSIA information can be obtained
at www.ICGtesting.com
Printed in the USA
LVHW051147160223
739655LV00005B/215

9 781177 919067